Auntie Emeleth's Astrology Grimoire

Emeleth Morliniel

Woolmonger Publishing

Dedication

To whoever writes that horoscope I've been gettin in my email every day for the past decade. You are wicked accurate!

Table of Contents

Introduction to Astrology and Witchcraft

The intersection of astrology and witchcraft creates a rich tapestry of spiritual practice, where celestial influences and magical intentions harmoniously intertwine. Both disciplines offer profound insights into the self and the universe, making them complementary tools for personal growth and empowerment. Understanding how astrology informs witchcraft and vice versa enhances the practitioner's ability to tap into universal energies, enabling a deeper connection to their spiritual journey.

Astrological spellcasting represents a fusion of zodiac characteristics with specific rituals designed to resonate with the unique traits of each sign. For instance, a spell aimed at enhancing creativity may be particularly powerful when performed under the influence of Leo, known for its artistic flair. By aligning intentions with the energies of different zodiac signs, practitioners can amplify their spells, making them more effective. Exploring the specific traits and elements associated with each sign allows for the creation of tailored rituals that not only honor astrological influences but also engage personal intentions.

Alongside spellcasting, astrology serves as a powerful tool for divination. Astrological charts can provide insights into future events and personal challenges, guiding practitioners in their magical pursuits. Techniques such as horary astrology, which answers specific questions based on the positions of celestial bodies at the time the question is posed, can be invaluable for witches seeking clarity in their practices. By integrating astrological insights into divination methods, practitioners can gain a deeper understanding of the energies at play in their lives, allowing for more informed decision-making when it comes to their magical work.

Astrological rituals for manifestation use specific celestial events to focus intentions and desires. For example, eclipses and planetary transits offer potent opportunities for transformation and change. By creating rituals that align with these cosmic occurrences, practitioners can magnify their manifestation efforts. Rituals might include crafting intention candles, performing guided meditations, or invoking elemental energies associated with the astrological event. Such practices not only deepen the connection to the universe but also empower individuals to take an active role in shaping their destinies.

The concept of elemental astrology adds another layer to the practice of witchcraft, highlighting the relationships between the four elements—earth, air, fire, and water—and the zodiac signs. Each sign is associated with one of these elements, influencing its characteristics and energies. By understanding these elemental connections, practitioners can incorporate the appropriate elemental energies into their rituals and spells. Additionally, using zodiac-based crystals and gemstones can further enhance magical practices, as each stone resonates with the energy of specific signs. This synergy between astrology and witchcraft not only enriches individual practices but also fosters a deeper understanding of the interconnectedness of all things in the cosmos.

Understanding the Zodiac Signs and Their Energies

Zodiac signs serve as a profound lens through which we can explore the energies that influence our lives and the universe around us. Each sign is imbued with unique characteristics, qualities, and elemental associations that shape our personalities, behaviors, and interactions. Understanding these energies is essential for anyone engaged in astrology and witchcraft, as it allows practitioners to align their magical practices with the celestial influences that govern their existence. By recognizing the traits associated with each sign, individuals can tailor their rituals and spells to use the most potent energies available.

Astrology is intricately linked with elemental forces, as each zodiac sign corresponds to one of the four elements: earth, air, fire, or water. Earth signs (Taurus, Virgo, Capricorn) embody stability, practicality, and a connection to nature, making them ideal for grounding rituals and manifestation practices. Air signs (Gemini, Libra, Aquarius) are associated with intellect, communication, and creativity, which can enhance divination techniques and spellcasting that require mental clarity. Fire signs (Aries, Leo, Sagittarius) exude passion, energy, and transformation, making them powerful allies for spells aimed at invoking change or ambition. Lastly, water signs (Cancer, Scorpio, Pisces) embody intuition, emotion, and healing, providing an essential foundation for rituals that seek emotional balance and spiritual insight.

Including zodiac energies into spellcasting is not only an art but also a science that can significantly amplify the effectiveness of one's magical practices. Each sign's ruling planet further influences its energies, providing additional layers of understanding. For example, a spell for courage and confidence would be particularly potent during the transit of Aries, ruled by Mars. By aligning spells with the zodiac signs and their planetary rulers, practitioners can create a synergy that enhances their intentions and outcomes. This alignment is crucial for anyone looking to deepen their connection to the astrological forces at play and maximize their magical potential.

Astrological rituals can also be designed to coincide with significant celestial events, such as eclipses, new moons, or planetary transits. These moments in time are charged with unique energies that can be used for personal growth and manifestation. For instance, a ritual performed during a lunar eclipse can be particularly powerful for releasing old patterns and embracing new beginnings, especially for those with strong connections to the signs of Cancer or Capricorn. By understanding the cyclical nature of astrology and its impact on personal energy, practitioners can cultivate a dynamic relationship with the cosmos, allowing their rituals to reflect the ever-changing landscape of the universe.

Using crystals and gemstones that resonate with the appropriate zodiac signs adds another layer of depth to astrological practices. Each sign vibes with specific stones that enhance its energies and attributes, aiding in both magical and healing endeavors. For example, Taurus individuals may benefit from the grounding properties of rose quartz, while Scorpios might utilize labradorite for its transformative qualities. By including these gemstones into rituals or wearing them as talismans, practitioners can amplify their intentions and create a harmonious balance between their astrological influences and personal energies. Understanding zodiac signs and their energies is not merely an exploration of personality traits but a pathway to using the profound forces of the universe for personal empowerment and spiritual growth.

The Importance of Rituals and Spells

Rituals and spells hold a central place in the practices of astrology and witchcraft, serving as tangible expressions of intention and belief. These practices allow individuals to connect with the cosmos, using celestial energies that resonate with their zodiac signs. Each ritual or spell is a unique blend of personal intention and universal energy, providing a framework for manifestation that aligns with astrological influences. By understanding the importance of rituals and spells, practitioners can enhance their spiritual journeys, tap into the divine, and create meaningful transformations in their lives.

Astrological spellcasting combines the inherent traits and energies of zodiac signs with specific spells designed to amplify their effects. Each sign possesses distinct characteristics; for instance, Aries is associated with action and courage, while Pisces embodies intuition and emotional depth. By aligning spells with these traits, practitioners can create a more potent and personalized experience. This alignment not only increases the likelihood of success but also fosters a deeper connection between the practitioner and the celestial influences at play. Understanding the nuances of each zodiac sign enhances the effectiveness of spellcasting, allowing for a more profound relationship with the energies that govern the universe.

Along with spellcasting, astrology serves as a powerful tool for divination. Techniques that utilize astrological charts for predictive purposes can provide insights into future events and personal growth. By examining transits, progressions, and natal charts, practitioners can gain clarity on their life path and the influences surrounding them. This divine guidance can inform the creation of rituals that align with specific astrological events, such as eclipses or planetary transits, enabling individuals to manifest their intentions more effectively. The integration of astrology into divination practices enriches the experience, providing a roadmap for spiritual development and self-discovery.

Astrological rituals for manifestation are particularly potent when aligned with significant celestial events. Eclipses, for example, are powerful moments of transformation, representing endings and new beginnings. By crafting rituals that use the energies of these events, practitioners can create a sacred space for setting intentions and manifesting desires. The timing of such rituals is crucial; performing them during specific astrological phases can amplify their effectiveness, aligning personal goals with the cosmic rhythm. Whether focusing on personal growth, love, or abundance, these rituals serve as a catalyst for change, providing a structured approach to using the universe's energies.

The elemental aspect of astrology adds another layer of depth to rituals and spells. Each zodiac sign is associated with one of the four elements: earth, air, fire, or water, each embodying unique qualities and energies. Understanding these elemental associations can inform the choice of materials, symbols, and actions taken during rituals. For instance, an earth sign like Taurus may benefit from grounding rituals using stones or herbs, while a fire sign like Leo may find empowerment through candle spells. Additionally, zodiac-based crystals and gemstones can enhance magical and healing practices, allowing practitioners to tap into the vibrational energies that resonate with their astrological identities. By integrating these elements into their rituals and spells, individuals can create a harmonious practice that honors both their personal astrological influences and the greater cosmic tapestry.

The Traits of Each Zodiac Sign

Aries: The Pioneer

In the realm of astrology, Aries stands as the embodiment of pioneering spirit and unyielding courage. As the first sign of the zodiac, represented by the ram, Aries individuals are known for their boldness, enthusiasm, and a strong desire to forge their own paths. This fire sign, ruled by Mars, the planet of action and desire, ignites the passion and motivation necessary to embark on new adventures. Those born under this sign typically exhibit a natural inclination towards leadership and a willingness to take risks, making them the trailblazers of the zodiac. Understanding these intrinsic traits can significantly enhance the practice of rituals and spells tailored for Aries, allowing practitioners to use their dynamic energy effectively.

When it comes to astrological spellcasting, Aries energy can be directed toward manifesting ambition and personal growth. Rituals that emphasize initiation and courage resonate well with this fiery sign. A simple yet powerful spell for Aries involves crafting a passion jar filled with red candles, cinnamon, and a sprinkle of cayenne pepper—elements that symbolize energy and motivation. Lighting the candles while focusing on personal goals can amplify the intent, channeling the pioneering vigor of Aries into tangible outcomes. Additionally, including affirmations that reflect an Aries' fearless nature can further enhance the effectiveness of the spell, aligning personal desires with the universe's energies.

Divination techniques can also benefit from the assertiveness of Aries. Utilizing astrological charts during a new moon phase can provide clarity on upcoming ventures or personal aspirations. Aries individuals thrive on action and decisiveness, making tarot readings focused on movement and change particularly effective. By combining the directness of Aries with the intuitive insights of tarot, practitioners can unveil paths that align with their pioneering spirit. This approach not only guides individuals in their current endeavors but also empowers them to make confident choices in their journeys.

Incorporating elemental astrology into rituals for Aries can deepen the connection with their inherent fire element. Rituals that engage the element of fire—such as bonfires or candlelit ceremonies—can invigorate Aries energy, promoting transformation and release. For instance, during a fire ceremony, practitioners can write down fears or obstacles on parchment and burn them, symbolizing the release of limitations. This act not only channels the assertive energy of Aries but also reinforces the sign's association with renewal and rebirth, allowing individuals to emerge stronger and more focused.

Using crystals and gemstones can support the energetic needs of Aries. Red jasper, garnet, and carnelian are particularly resonant for those born under this sign, promoting vitality, courage, and confidence. Incorporating these stones into rituals, whether worn as jewelry or placed on an altar, can enhance the fiery energy that Aries embodies. During manifestation rituals, holding these crystals while envisioning personal goals can amplify intentions, making the spellcasting process even more potent. By aligning with the unique traits and energies of Aries, practitioners can unlock their potential as pioneers in both their spiritual and everyday lives.

Taurus: The Builder

Taurus, often referred to as "The Builder," embodies the essence of stability, practicality, and determination. Ruled by Venus, this earth sign is deeply connected to the physical world, making it a powerhouse of manifestation and creation. Individuals born under Taurus are known for their reliability and strong work ethic, which allows them to cultivate their dreams into reality. In the realm of astrology and witchcraft, using the energies of Taurus can significantly enhance your ability to manifest desires, build solid foundations, and create lasting transformations in your life.

Incorporating Taurus energy into your rituals can be particularly beneficial during key astrological events, such as the Taurus new moon or the Venus transits. These periods are ideal for setting intentions related to abundance, security, and personal growth. One effective ritual involves creating a sacred space adorned with elements associated with Taurus—such as earth tones, greenery, and gemstones like rose quartz and emerald. As you ground yourself in this space, visualize your goals taking shape, drawing upon the steadfast energy of Taurus to support and nurture your endeavors.

When it comes to spellcasting, Taurus individuals can benefit from specific spells that align with their traits. For instance, spells focused on financial growth, home stability, or personal beauty resonate deeply with Taurus' Venusian influence. Crafting a simple spell jar filled with herbs like basil for prosperity, cinnamon for warmth, and a piece of jade for abundance can create a powerful talisman. As you work with these ingredients, recite affirmations that reinforce your intentions, allowing the energy of Taurus to amplify your desires and bring them into fruition.

Astrological divination techniques can also be enhanced by understanding the Taurus archetype. By examining the position of Venus in your natal chart or in the charts of those you seek to read, you can gain insights into how Taurus energy influences personal relationships, financial matters, and creative pursuits. Utilizing astrological charts for predictive purposes can reveal patterns that align with Taurus traits, guiding you to leverage the strengths of this sign when making important decisions or navigating challenges.

The elemental connection of Taurus to the earth provides a solid foundation for various magical practices. Earth, as an element, signifies stability and support, making it essential for grounding rituals. Incorporating natural materials—such as soil, stones, or even plants—into your practices not only honors Taurus but also enhances the efficacy of your spells. By pairing these elements with Taurus-specific crystals, like smoky quartz or garnet, you can create a powerful synergy that amplifies your intentions, allowing you to build a life that reflects your deepest desires. Through understanding and channeling the energies of Taurus, you can use the power of "The Builder" to turn your dreams into tangible reality.

Certain crystals, herbs, plants, essential oils, and spell ingredients resonate more strongly with Aries than others. Notable stones include Carnelian, which boosts courage and motivation; Red Jasper, recognized for its grounding and energizing properties; Quartz, known for amplifying intentions and energy; Citrine, associated with prosperity and creativity; Garnet, a symbol of passion and vitality; and Hematite, which offers grounding and protective energy while aiding focus.

Among herbs, several align well with Aries' fiery spirit, such as Rosemary, which enhances clarity and is often used for purification; Dandelion, symbolizing resilience and strength; Thyme, known for its protective qualities and ability to inspire courage; Basil, linked to love and protection, making it excellent for attracting positive energy; Peppermint, an invigorating herb that boosts mental clarity; Cinnamon, often utilized for success and protection, adding warmth and passion; and Clove, recognized for its protective attributes and focus enhancement. Essential oils that complement Aries include Sweet Orange Essential Oil, which is uplifting and energizing, fostering joy and creativity; Bergamot Essential Oil, known for its calming effects while enhancing confidence; Ginger Essential Oil, stimulating and energizing, perfect for motivation; and Black Pepper Essential Oil, which strengthens courage and determination.

Other components for Aries spells might involve Chili Pepper, signifying passion and vitality, suitable for protection spells; the Fire Element, which symbolizes transformation and energy in rituals; and Sunstone, a crystal that embodies solar energy, promoting joy and vitality. These elements align well with the dynamic and assertive nature of Aries, enriching their traits and intentions in spells and rituals.

Gemini: The Communicator

In the complex workings of astrology, Gemini stands out as the quintessential communicator, a sign characterized by its duality, intellect, and vivacious spirit. Governed by Mercury, the planet of communication, Gemini embodies the air element, which influences its adaptability and social nature. Those born under this sign are often seen as the life of the party, possessing a natural charm and a gift for conversation. This duality not only enriches their interactions but also allows them to navigate various social landscapes with ease. In the realm of witchcraft, understanding Gemini's communicative essence opens the door to rituals and spells that use their unique energy for personal transformation and interpersonal relationships.

Gemini's communicative traits make it an ideal sign for spells centered around dialogue, negotiation, and clarity. When seeking to improve communication in relationships, whether romantic, platonic, or professional, one can create a ritual that incorporates the energies of Gemini. This can involve setting intentions during a waxing moon, when growth and new beginnings are favored. Using tools such as blue candles, symbolizing clarity, and fresh flowers to represent the sign's love for life, practitioners can call upon Gemini's influence to enhance their ability to express themselves and understand others. Such rituals serve to align one's intentions with the dynamic and stimulating energy of Gemini, fostering a space where open dialogue can flourish.

In terms of divination, Gemini's association with Mercury also lends itself to various astrological techniques that can enhance intuitive abilities. Methods such as tarot readings or scrying can be enriched by considering the position of Mercury in one's natal chart. For instance, during Mercury retrograde, practitioners might find it beneficial to engage in reflective practices, such as journaling or meditative visualization, to gain insights into past communications and decisions. By aligning these divinatory practices with astrological events, individuals can deepen their understanding of their own thoughts and feelings, as well as those of others, leading to more profound revelations.

Using Gemini's air element is also essential for manifestation rituals. This sign thrives on movement and change, making it ideal for practices aimed at initiating new projects or ideas. Rituals conducted during Gemini season can incorporate elements like incense or feathers to represent air, facilitating the flow of new thoughts and inspirations. Setting intentions during this time can be particularly powerful; practitioners can write their desires on paper and release them into the wind, symbolizing the release of those intentions into the universe. By invoking Gemini's energy, one can manifest clarity and communication in their pursuits, ensuring that their goals are not only envisioned but also articulated and pursued with vigor.

Selecting the right crystals and gemstones can amplify the communicative strengths of Gemini. Stones such as aquamarine, which promotes clear communication, and labradorite, known for its ability to enhance psychic abilities and intuition, resonate well with this sign. Incorporating these crystals into daily rituals or carrying them during important conversations can help individuals use the positive attributes of Gemini. Additionally, creating a crystal grid focused on communication can serve as a powerful tool for amplifying intentions and connecting with the energies of this dynamic sign. By integrating these practices into their spiritual toolkit, practitioners can leverage the communicative prowess of Gemini to enhance their personal and spiritual growth.

Certain spell ingredients that are appropriate for Gemini and play to their strengths. Crystals include

Agate (particularly Blue Lace Agate), Citrine, Aquamarine, Clear Quartz, Moonstone, Labradorite, Sodalite.

The best herbs and plants for Gemini are Lavender, Peppermint, Dandelion, Rosemary, Chamomile, Elderflower, Sage. Essential oils perfect for Gemini would be lemon, Bergamot, Eucalyptus, Basil, Peppermint, Frankincense, and grapefruit. Other Spell Ingredients that work well for Geminis are Incense (such as sandalwood or jasmine), Paper and pen for writing intentions, Feathers (symbolizing air and communication), Crystals for communication (like Blue Kyanite), A small bell (to signify clarity and alertness). These ingredients resonate with Gemini's characteristics of communication, intellect, and adaptability.

Cancer: The Nurturer

Cancer, ruled by the Moon and belonging to the Water element, embodies the essence of nurturing, emotional depth, and intuitive wisdom. Those born under this sign are often seen as the caregivers of the zodiac, possessing an innate ability to understand and support others. This nurturing quality extends beyond personal relationships and into the realm of spiritual practices, making Cancer individuals particularly adept at creating rituals and spells that foster healing and emotional resilience. In this subchapter, we will explore how to use the nurturing energy of Cancer for personal growth, divination, and manifestation, as well as the significance of specific crystals that resonate with this sign.

In astrological spellcasting, Cancer's emotional intelligence can be utilized to create powerful rituals that focus on healing and protection. Incorporating elements such as water, moonlight, and nurturing herbs like chamomile and lavender can enhance the effectiveness of spells aimed at fostering a sense of safety and comfort. A simple yet potent ritual could involve crafting a protection pouch filled with these herbs, charging it under the light of a full moon while visualizing a protective barrier enveloping you or a loved one. This ritual not only connects with Cancer's nurturing nature but also invokes the Moon's energy, amplifying the power of the intention set forth.

For those interested in divination, Cancer's intuitive faculties can be used to interpret astrological charts and predict future events. Utilizing techniques such as lunar astrology, practitioners can examine the positions of the Moon in relation to personal natal charts to gain insight into emotional cycles and potential challenges. By paying attention to the Moon's phases, individuals can align their divination practices with the ebb and flow of lunar energy, enhancing their ability to read the signs and symbols that arise during readings. This approach not only deepens one's understanding of personal circumstances but also strengthens the connection to the nurturing qualities of Cancer.

Manifestation rituals during significant astrological events can be particularly powerful when aligned with Cancer's energies. The New Moon, symbolizing new beginnings, offers a prime opportunity for Cancer individuals to set intentions focused on emotional healing, self-care, or familial bonds. Creating a sacred space with elements that evoke comfort—such as soft fabrics, candles, and soothing scents—can enhance the experience. Writing intentions on biodegradable paper and releasing them into water symbolizes the flow of emotions and the nurturing aspect of Cancer, allowing these desires to be carried forth into the universe.

Crystals and gemstones associated with Cancer, such as moonstone, rose quartz, and aquamarine, can amplify the nurturing energies of this sign. Moonstone, in particular, resonates with the lunar influence, promoting intuition and emotional balance. Incorporating these stones into rituals, whether through meditation, carrying them in a pocket, or placing them on an altar, can deepen the connection to Cancer's nurturing essence. Additionally, using these crystals during spellcasting can help to ground the energies being called upon, promoting a sense of calm and emotional stability throughout the process. Embracing the nurturing qualities of Cancer not only enriches one's spiritual practice but also fosters a deeper understanding of the profound connections we share with ourselves and others.

The spell ingredients that align well with Cancer's nurturing nature include various stones and herbs. Stones such as Moonstone enhance intuition and emotional balance, while Rose Quartz promotes love, compassion, and emotional healing. Selenite is known for cleansing energy and providing clarity, whereas Carnelian boosts motivation and emotional stability. Clear Quartz amplifies energy and intentions, Labradorite offers protection and enhances intuition, and Amethyst brings calmness and spiritual insight.

For herbs, Jasmine is linked to love, intuition, and dreams, and Chamomile helps soothe emotions and encourages relaxation. Hibiscus enhances love and passion, while Mugwort supports dreams and intuition. Lavender calms the mind and fosters emotional balance, Lemon Balm uplifts mood and aids in emotional healing, Basil promotes love and protection, and Peppermint refreshes and invigorates the spirit.

Other useful ingredients for Cancerians include Coconut Oil, which is utilized in rituals for emotional healing and protection, Sage for cleansing negativity and promoting healing, Aloe Vera for its healing and protective properties, Frankincense Essential Oil to enhance meditation and spiritual connection, and Neroli Essential Oil for relaxation and emotional healing. These ingredients can be incorporated into spells, rituals, or personal wellness practices to embody the nurturing and intuitive essence of the Cancer zodiac sign.

Leo: The Leader

In the realm of astrology, Leo stands out as a beacon of leadership and charisma, embodying the vibrant energy of the fire element. Those born under this sign are often characterized by their innate ability to inspire and motivate others, making them natural leaders. This subchapter, "Leo: The Leader," delves into the astrological traits that contribute to Leo's commanding presence and explores how these qualities can be used in witchcraft and magical practices. Understanding the essence of Leo can empower practitioners to create rituals and spells that align with this sign's dynamic energy, enabling them to manifest their personal goals and elevate their spiritual journeys.

Leos are ruled by the Sun, which not only influences their radiant personality but also enhances their creative and expressive nature. This solar connection imbues them with a strong sense of self and an unwavering confidence that draws others to them. In astrological spellcasting, the energy of the Sun can be tapped into for rituals aimed at boosting self-esteem, igniting creativity, or attracting recognition. By including solar-themed elements, such as the colors gold and yellow, or using specific herbs like sunflower or calendula, practitioners can amplify their spells' effectiveness, channeling Leo's vibrant essence to achieve their desired outcomes.

In the context of divination, Leos can provide profound insights through their intuitive abilities. Their natural inclination to lead often translates into a keen understanding of others, allowing them to read situations and people well. Techniques like tarot readings or scrying can be enhanced by focusing on Leo's traits, using fire-based divination tools or crystals such as citrine and carnelian, which resonate with Leo's fiery nature. This combination can lead to more accurate predictions and revelations, guiding practitioners in their personal and spiritual endeavors while leveraging Leo's innate strengths.

Rituals for manifestation during significant astrological events can be particularly powerful for Leos. Eclipses, full moons, and solar events are ideal times for Leos to perform rituals that align with their goals of leadership, creativity, and personal growth. Incorporating symbols of the lion, such as lion figurines or imagery, along with fiery elements like candles or incense, can enhance the energy of these rituals. Practitioners can also set intentions that reflect Leo's qualities—such as courage, ambition, and generosity—inviting these attributes into their lives as they align with the cosmic energies present during these celestial events.

Finally, the connection between Leo and specific crystals can further enrich magical practices. Stones like amber, tiger's eye, and sunstone not only resonate with Leo's vibrant energy but also serve as powerful tools for manifestation and protection. By wearing or carrying these stones during rituals or daily activities, individuals can amplify their leadership qualities and attract opportunities that align with their aspirations. In combining the astrological insights of Leo with practical witchcraft techniques, practitioners can use the lion's strength, ensuring their personal and spiritual paths are illuminated by the radiant energy of this dynamic zodiac sign.

Leo has a big personality, and as such there are some spell ingredients that will resonate better with them. Some crystals include Citrine - Promotes confidence and happiness, Sunstone - Enhances vitality and joy, Tiger's Eye - Boosts courage and personal power, Carnelian - Stimulates creativity and passion, Amber - Represents warmth and protection, Gold - Symbolizes wealth and success, often used in rituals for abundance.

Herbs that really vibe with Leo are Marigold - Known for attracting positive energy and prosperity,

Sunflower - Represents warmth, loyalty, and positivity, Basil - Associated with love and protection, often used in spells for success, Ginger - Energizing and stimulating, promotes passion and motivation. There's also Clove - Enhances protection and strength in spells, Sage - Cleansing properties that promote clarity and peace, Peppermint - Stimulates the mind and enhances clarity, Pine - Represents resilience and strength, often used for purification, Lemon Balm - Brings joy and calms the mind, Cardamom - Stimulates creativity and confidence, Hibiscus Flower - Associated with love and passion, often used in love spells.

For essential oils, Leos can't beat Lemon - Uplifting and energizing, good for clarity and joy, Orange - Encourages enthusiasm and creativity, Rosemary - Boosts memory and clarity, often used for protection. These ingredients can be used in various rituals, spellwork, or simply kept nearby to use the Leo energy of confidence, creativity, and warmth.

Virgo: The Analyst

Virgo, the sixth sign of the zodiac, is symbolized by the Maiden and is associated with the Earth element. Individuals born under this sign, from August 23 to September 22, are known for their analytical minds, attention to detail, and practicality.

Virgos possess a unique ability to dissect information and situations, making them adept at problem-solving. This analytical nature extends into their spiritual practices, as they seek to understand the deeper meanings behind rituals, spells, and astrological influences. In this subchapter, we will explore how Virgos can use their innate qualities in their astrological and witchcraft practices, enhancing their connection to both the physical and metaphysical realms.

When it comes to astrological spellcasting, Virgos thrive on the precision and clarity that their analytical minds provide. They are drawn to spells that require meticulous planning and execution, often preferring rituals that incorporate detailed lists or structured methodologies. A powerful spell for a Virgo may involve creating a comprehensive vision board, where they can visualize their goals with clarity, supported by their innate organizational skills. By combining the meticulous nature of Virgo with astrological insights, practitioners can create spells tailored to specific lunar phases or planetary alignments, ensuring that their intentions are aligned with the universe's energies.

In the realm of divination, Virgos can excel by utilizing their analytical prowess to interpret astrological charts. Methods such as natal chart readings, transits, and progressions can be profoundly insightful for them. By approaching divination with a critical eye, Virgos can uncover layers of meaning in their readings that others may overlook. Journaling these insights can also be beneficial, allowing Virgos to track their progress and reflect on their spiritual journey over time. This analytical approach not only enhances their divination practice but also empowers them to make informed decisions based on cosmic influences.

Elemental astrology plays a significant role in Virgo's spiritual practices, as they are an Earth sign. This connection to the Earth element encourages Virgos to engage in rituals that ground and stabilize their energies. Earth-based rituals, such as working with soil, planting seeds, or creating herbal sachets, can help Virgos channel their analytical abilities into tangible forms of magic. Incorporating elements like stones and crystals, particularly those aligned with Virgo's traits—such as carnelian for motivation or sodalite for clarity—can enhance their rituals and amplify their intentions. These practices not only align with their earthy nature but also allow them to manifest their desires effectively.

Ultimately, the analytical traits of Virgo serve as a robust foundation for their astrological and witchcraft practices. By embracing their inherent qualities, Virgos can create meaningful rituals and spells that resonate with their true selves. The combination of analytical thinking, attention to detail, and an Earth-centered approach to spirituality allows Virgos to manifest their goals and navigate life's challenges with greater ease. As they delve deeper into the realms of astrology and witchcraft, they will find that their analytical skills are not just tools for understanding the world around them but also pathways to profound personal transformation and spiritual growth.

Certain spell components resonate strongly with Virgo's attention to detail and refined tastes, such as Amethyst, Carnelian, Jade, Fluorite, Hematite, Green Aventurine, Amazonite, and Clear Quartz. Virgos also appreciate herbs and plants, making Lavender, Peppermint, Chamomile, Sage, Thyme, Dandelion, Oregano, and Basil ideal selections. The essential oils that align well with them include Frankincense, Rosemary, Eucalyptus, Lavender, Tea Tree, Lemon, and Bergamot. Furthermore, some spell ingredients that align perfectly with Virgo traits are Sea Salt (for purification), Honey (for sweetness and harmony), Cinnamon (for abundance and protection), and Cloves (for protection and strength). These components reflect Virgo's practical nature, meticulousness, and profound connection to the natural world.

Libra: The Harmonizer

Libra, represented by the scales, embodies the essence of harmony, balance, and diplomacy. This air sign is ruled by Venus, the planet of love and beauty, which enhances its natural ability to foster relationships and create equilibrium in various aspects of life. Those born under the sign of Libra often possess a keen sense of justice and a desire for peace, making them natural mediators. In the realm of astrology and witchcraft, using the energies of Libra can be particularly beneficial for rituals focused on partnership, social connections, and aesthetic pursuits. By understanding the characteristics of Libra, practitioners can create spells and rituals that align with this sign's unique attributes.

When focusing on astrological spellcasting, Libras thrive in environments that promote collaboration and mutual understanding. Spells that encourage cooperation among individuals or groups are especially potent during the Libra season, which occurs from late September to late October. Incorporating elements associated with Libra, such as the colors pink and green, or symbols like the scale and the dove, can enhance the efficacy of these spells. Practicing rituals during key astrological events, such as the full moon in Libra, can also amplify the intention behind the spell, allowing for a greater manifestation of balance and harmony in one's life.

In divination, Libra's influence can aid in revealing insights related to relationships and interpersonal dynamics. Utilizing astrological charts, practitioners can analyze the placement of Venus and other significant planetary alignments to gain deeper understanding of romantic partnerships, friendships, and professional collaborations. Techniques such as tarot readings can be enriched by including Libra's attributes, focusing on questions that pertain to fairness, beauty, and balance. This blend of astrology and divination not only fosters a deeper connection with the divine but also empowers individuals to navigate their social paths more effectively.

Manifestation rituals rooted in Libra's energy can be particularly transformative, especially when designed to attract love, friendship, or harmony. Rituals that coincide with astrological events, like the equinox or lunar phases, can create powerful opportunities for manifesting equilibrium in one's life. Incorporating elements like candle magic, where pink or green candles represent love and balance, can enhance the ritual's effectiveness. Additionally, using crystals such as rose quartz, which resonates with Libra's love-driven energy, can amplify intentions during these practices, helping to align one's desires with the universal flow of harmony.

Understanding Libra's elemental association with air allows practitioners to explore its connections with other elements in their magical practices. Air represents intellect, communication, and social interaction, making it vital for spells and rituals focused on clarity in relationships and the expression of love. By integrating elemental astrology into their work, practitioners can create a balanced approach that honors the air element while also considering the influence of earth, fire, and water. This holistic understanding enhances the overall effectiveness of Libra-inspired spells, allowing for a richer, more nuanced approach to achieving harmony and balance in all areas of life.

Libra, ruled by Venus, is associated with balance, harmony, beauty, and relationships. Here are only some of the spell ingredients that resonate with Libra's energy. Rose Quartz Promotes love and emotional healing. Lapis Lazuli Enhances communication and self-expression. Celestite Encourages peace and tranquility. Aquamarine Supports clarity in relationships and emotional balance. Selenite Cleanses and purifies energy, promoting harmony. Jade Attracts prosperity and fosters balance. Moonstone Enhances intuition and emotional stability.

Lavender Calms the mind and promotes relaxation. Rosemary is Used for protection and purification, also symbolizes remembrance. Chamomile Brings peace and relaxation, often used in love spells. Mint Invigorates and uplifts the spirit, attracting positive energy. Basil is Associated with love and harmony in relationships. Ylang Ylang Promotes love, sensuality, and emotional balance, Geranium - Supports emotional stability and healing, Bergamot - Uplifting and calming, great for promoting joy, Sage - Used for cleansing and protection, helps balance energies, Frankincense - Enhances meditation and spiritual awareness., Citrine - Attracts abundance, success, and positivity.

Other spell ingredients that suit Libra's aesthetic penchant are Himalayan Salt which purifies energy and creates a peaceful environment, and certain Candle Colors - Pink for love, blue for peace, and green for balance. These ingredients can be used in various spells, rituals, or meditation practices to use the harmonious and relational energies that Libra embodies.

Scorpio: The Transformer

Scorpio, the eighth sign of the zodiac, is often referred to as the Transformer due to its profound ability to navigate the depths of emotional and spiritual transformation. Governed by the element of Water, Scorpios are known for their intense passion, deep emotional currents, and an innate capacity for regeneration. This sign's association with the transformative process can be seen in its ruling planet, Pluto, which symbolizes death, rebirth, and the cycles of life. In the realm of astrology and witchcraft, Scorpios embody the essence of metamorphosis, making them powerful allies in rituals aimed at personal growth and transformation.

The energy of Scorpio is inherently linked to

themes of power, secrecy, and the hidden aspects of the psyche. This sign thrives on exploring the shadows, prompting practitioners to delve into their inner worlds, confront fears, and emerge renewed. For those engaging in astrological spellcasting, invoking Scorpio's transformative energy can facilitate significant shifts in one's life. Effective spells may involve elements that resonate with Scorpio's nature, such as those focusing on shedding old patterns or embracing new identities. Utilizing candles in deep red or black, which symbolize passion and protection, can enhance these energies and amplify the results of your intentions.

In the context of divination, Scorpio's depth offers a unique advantage. Techniques such as astrology-based tarot readings can be particularly potent when aligned with Scorpio's transformative qualities. By examining astrological charts during significant lunar phases or eclipses, practitioners can tap into the potential for change that Scorpio embodies. Such moments can serve as powerful catalysts for divination, allowing individuals to unearth hidden truths and gain insights necessary for their personal evolution. This alignment not only enhances the clarity of the reading but also aligns the practitioner with the cyclical nature of transformation inherent in Scorpio.

Rituals designed for manifestation often benefit from Scorpio's intense energy. For instance, conducting a ritual during a Scorpio new moon can be a potent time to set intentions related to transformation, healing, and empowerment. Participants might create a sacred space with water elements—such as bowls of water or a small fountain—to symbolize the fluidity and adaptability of Scorpio. Incorporating herbs like mugwort and black cohosh, known for their protective and transformative properties, can further enhance the ritual. By harmonizing the energies of the moment with the characteristics of Scorpio, practitioners can effectively channel their desires for profound personal change.

This sign's water element plays a crucial role in its transformative abilities. Water symbolizes emotions, intuition, and the subconscious—areas where Scorpios excel. Crystals such as obsidian, labradorite, and moonstone resonate deeply with Scorpio's energies, serving as tools for grounding, protection, and intuitive insight. Whether used in meditation, spellwork, or simply worn as jewelry, these stones can amplify the transformative qualities of Scorpio, allowing practitioners to connect more deeply with their emotional depths and facilitate healing. By understanding and using the transformative power of Scorpio, individuals can embark on a journey of self-discovery and empowerment, embracing the profound changes that lie ahead.

These are some crystals, herbs, plants, essential

oils, and other spell ingredients that align well with the intense and transformative energy of Scorpio. For crystals, consider Black Obsidian for protection and grounding, Malachite to support emotional healing and transformation, Garnet to enhance passion and revitalize energy, Bloodstone to aid in courage and strength during challenges, Aquamarine to promote calmness and clarity in emotional matters, Carnelian to boost motivation and creativity, and Selenite for clarity and spiritual insight. Herbs that resonate with Scorpio's intensity include Rosemary for purification and protection, Sage for cleansing and releasing negative energy, Basil to enhance love and prosperity, Dill for support in protection and dispelling negativity, and Mugwort for aiding dreams and intuition.

When it comes to essential oils, Patchouli Essential Oil encourages sensuality and grounding, Frankincense Essential Oil promotes spiritual awareness and meditation, Cypress Essential Oil offers emotional balance and transformation, and Ylang-Ylang Essential Oil enhances love and emotional healing. Other spell ingredients that Scorpio may find appealing are Juniper Berries for protection and purification, Hibiscus for attracting love and passion, Pine Needles for cleansing and bringing clarity, and Nettle for providing support in protection and strength. These ingredients can be utilized in various ways, including spells, rituals, or simply to enhance personal energy that aligns with Scorpio's characteristics.

Sagittarius: The Explorer

Sagittarius, the ninth sign of the zodiac, is often celebrated as the Explorer, embodying a spirit of adventure, curiosity, and a quest for knowledge. Governed by Jupiter, the planet of expansion and abundance, Sagittarians are drawn to travel, philosophy, and the pursuit of truth. This sign is associated with the fire element, which fuels their enthusiasm and desire for exploration. Those born under this sign are not just wanderers; they are seekers of deeper meaning, constantly in search of new experiences that broaden their horizons and enhance their understanding of the world.

In the realm of astrological spellcasting, leveraging the energies of Sagittarius can be particularly potent for rituals aimed at personal growth and exploration. Spells that focus on adventure, learning, and self-discovery can be enhanced by using the vibrant energy of Sagittarius. For instance, a ritual involving the lighting of a candle infused with scents of cinnamon and frankincense can help to ignite the Sagittarian spirit, promoting a sense of wanderlust and encouraging the practitioner to step outside their comfort zone. Incorporating elements such as maps or travel journals into the spell can further align the ritual with the exploratory nature of this sign.

For those interested in divination, Sagittarius offers unique insights through astrological charts. The sign's association with higher learning and philosophy means that divinatory practices can benefit from its expansive nature. Techniques such as astrological tarot readings can be particularly effective when the moon is in Sagittarius, as this placement enhances intuition and the ability to see the bigger picture. Additionally, practitioners can utilize Sagittarius energy during planetary transits to explore questions related to travel, education, and personal beliefs, allowing for a deeper understanding of their life path.

Manifestation rituals rooted in Sagittarius energies can be powerful tools for personal development. Timing these rituals to coincide with key astrological events, such as a full moon in Sagittarius, can amplify their effects. A simple yet effective ritual might involve writing down goals related to travel or new experiences and placing them under a piece of amethyst or lapis lazuli—two stones that resonate with the Sagittarian spirit. As the waxing moon encourages growth, practitioners can visualize their desires taking flight, supported by the expansive and optimistic energy of Sagittarius.

Incorporating the elemental aspects of Sagittarius into witchcraft practices can deepen one's connection to this sign. Since Sagittarius is a fire sign, elements of warmth, passion, and transformation are integral to its energy. Utilizing fire in rituals—such as burning sage or lighting candles—can help channel the assertive and liberating qualities of Sagittarius. Furthermore, engaging with specific crystals like turquoise or citrine can enhance the exploration of new ideas and experiences, providing the wearer with both protection and encouragement on their journey. Through a harmonious blend of astrology, witchcraft, and personal intention, individuals can unlock the true potential of Sagittarius as the ultimate explorer.

Sagittarius has lofty aspirations, and their spell components need to reflect their adventurous spirit. Crystals that resonate well with Sagittarius include Amethyst, which enhances intuition and spiritual awareness; Turquoise, known for promoting communication and self-expression; Citrine, which encourages abundance and positivity; Lapis Lazuli, aiding in deepening philosophical understanding; Topaz, enhancing creativity and intellectual pursuits; and Sodalite, which boosts rational thought and emotional balance.

Herbs that complement Sagittarius are Ginger, which stimulates energy and motivation; Dandelion, symbolizing resilience and freedom; Clove, invoking protection and strength; Peppermint, refreshing the mind and body to support clarity; Frankincense, promoting spiritual growth and meditation; Sage, used for cleansing and purification; Basil, associated with prosperity and good fortune; and Rosemary, enhancing memory and mental clarity. Bay Leaf, utilized for wishes and manifestations, and cardamom, which encourages optimism and joy, are also beneficial.

Ideal essential oils for Sagittarius include cedarwood essential oil for grounding and calming effects; grapefruit Essential Oil for an invigorating and uplifting experience; Cinnamon, which attracts abundance and passion; and Jasmine, known for enhancing creativity and inspiring spiritual growth. These elements embody the adventurous, optimistic, and philosophical traits of Sagittarius, making them perfect for spells and rituals linked to this zodiac sign.

Capricorn: The Achiever

Capricorn, symbolized by the steadfast goat, embodies the qualities of determination, ambition, and practicality. As the achiever of the zodiac, Capricorns are known for their ability to set goals and relentlessly pursue them until they reach the pinnacle of success. This Earth sign is ruled by Saturn, the planet associated with discipline, responsibility, and structure. These traits make Capricorn individuals not only effective in their endeavors but also adept at laying a solid foundation for their dreams. In astrology and witchcraft, understanding the energies of Capricorn can significantly enhance rituals and spells aimed at manifestation and personal growth.

To use the powerful energies of Capricorn in your magical practices, consider creating rituals that align with the sign's characteristics. A Capricorn-focused ritual can be particularly effective during significant astrological events, such as the winter solstice, which aligns with Capricorn's season. This time is ideal for setting intentions related to career, stability, and long-term goals. Incorporate elements such as earth-based offerings, like crystals and herbs, specifically chosen for their resonance with Capricorn's energies. Black tourmaline, garnet, and onyx are excellent crystals for this sign, known for their grounding properties and ability to enhance focus and determination.

Along with ritual work, Capricorn lends itself well to astrological spellcasting. When crafting spells, focus on themes of ambition, perseverance, and success. By utilizing specific planetary transits, such as when Saturn is in a favorable position, you can amplify your spell's potency. For example, casting a spell for career advancement during a Saturn transit can enhance your ability to manifest professional goals. Incorporate Capricorn symbols, like the mountain or the goat, into your spellwork to reinforce the connection to this sign's inherent energy of achievement.

Capricorn's earth element plays a vital role in elemental astrology and its relationship with witchcraft practices. Earth is associated with stability, practicality, and fertility, making it an excellent foundation for rituals aimed at material wealth and personal development. Incorporate natural elements such as soil, stones, or plants into your rituals to create a deeper connection with Capricorn's grounded energies. Meditating on the essence of the earth can help solidify your intentions and draw forth the resources needed to manifest your aspirations.

When considering using zodiac-based crystals, it's essential to recognize how these gemstones can enhance the qualities inherent to Capricorn. Crystals like smoky quartz and citrine can bolster a Capricorn's ability to manifest their desires while providing protection against negativity. Integrating these stones into your daily practices, whether through meditation, carrying them with you, or placing them on your altar, can create a harmonious flow of energy that supports your goals. By understanding the multifaceted nature of Capricorn, practitioners can unlock a wealth of potential in their astrological and magical endeavors, ultimately transforming ambition into tangible achievement.

Capricorn, governed by Saturn, embodies

qualities such as discipline, ambition, and practicality. To align with Capricorn's drive, specific spell ingredients are essential. Crystals that resonate with this sign include Black Tourmaline, Garnet, Onyx, Malachite, Fluorite, Hematite, Smoky Quartz, Tiger's Eye, Jet, and Green Aventurine. The most suitable herbs to capture Capricorn's elevated essence are Rosemary, Sage, Thyme, Basil, Dandelion, Cedar, Nettle, Juniper, Pine, and Mugwort. Essential oils that Capricorns might find beneficial are Cedarwood, Frankincense, Patchouli, Myrrh, and Bergamot. Additionally, items that complement Capricorn's spells include Sea Salt, Black Candles (symbolizing protection and grounding), Clay (representing stability and a connection to the earth), Iron Shavings (for strength and resilience), and Ashes (for transformation and release). These ingredients can be utilized in various spells, rituals, or as tools to amplify Capricorn's inherent qualities and energies.

Aquarius: The Visionary

Aquarius, the eleventh sign of the zodiac, embodies the spirit of innovation and humanitarianism, earning its moniker as "The Visionary." Ruled by Uranus, the planet of revolution and originality, Aquarians are known for their forward-thinking ideas and unique perspectives. This air sign thrives on intellectual stimulation and is often drawn to unconventional paths, making them natural leaders in social movements and change. Their connection to the collective consciousness allows them to tap into the zeitgeist, enabling them to envision a future that transcends the limitations of the present. In the context of astrology and witchcraft, exploring the traits of Aquarius can enhance both divination practices and spellcasting techniques.

When it comes to astrological spellcasting, using the energy of Aquarius can amplify intentions related to innovation and social justice. Rituals that align with the Aquarian archetype often focus on community, equality, and visionary goals. One effective spell involves creating a "Vision Board" during the Aquarius New Moon, a time when the energies of new beginnings are particularly potent. Gather images, words, and symbols that represent your aspirations for social change and personal growth. As you arrange your board, visualize the impact of your dreams on the world, invoking the Aquarian spirit to inspire your intentions. This practice not only serves to manifest personal desires but also aligns with the collective goals that Aquarians hold dear.

Divination techniques can also benefit from the visionary qualities of Aquarius. Astrological charts can be interpreted to reveal insights about future trends and collective movements. For instance, during significant transits involving Uranus, such as its retrograde phases, practitioners can perform divination to explore themes of innovation and disruption. Using tools like tarot or scrying, focus on the questions that resonate with the Aquarian ethos, such as how to contribute to societal evolution or how to embrace change in one's life. The insights gained during these divination sessions can help individuals align their personal actions with the greater good, fostering a deeper connection with the Aquarian vision of the future.

Manifestation rituals rooted in the elemental energies of Aquarius can further enhance one's practice. Being an air sign, Aquarius is associated with intellect, communication, and social interaction. Incorporating air elements into rituals—such as burning incense, using feathers, or engaging in breathwork—can help channel the sign's dynamic energy. A powerful ritual might involve writing down intentions on biodegradable paper and releasing them into the wind, symbolizing the dissemination of one's vision into the universe. This act not only honors the air element but also resonates with the Aquarian desire for freedom and exploration, allowing one's aspirations to take flight.

In addition to ritual and spellcasting, integrating zodiac-based crystals and gemstones can deepen one's connection to the energy of Aquarius. Stones like amethyst, aquamarine, and labradorite resonate with the visionary qualities of this sign. Amethyst enhances intuition and spiritual insight, making it a perfect companion for Aquarians seeking to refine their foresight. Aquamarine, known for its calming properties, can assist in facilitating clear communication, a key trait for Aquarian leaders. Labradorite, with its mystical aura, fosters creativity and transformation, empowering individuals to embrace their unique visions. By including these stones into daily practices—whether worn as jewelry, used in rituals, or meditated upon—individuals can enhance their connection to the visionary energies of Aquarius, further enriching their astrological and witchcraft journeys.

Aquarius is characterized by its visionary nature, and their spells require a unique touch. The crystals that resonate with this energy include Amethyst for enhancing intuition and spiritual growth, Aquamarine for promoting calmness and emotional clarity, Labradorite for encouraging transformation and shielding against negativity, Clear Quartz for amplifying energy and intention, Citrine for attracting prosperity and joy, Blue Lace Agate for facilitating communication and self-expression, Garnet for boosting energy and passion, Hematite for grounding and enhancing focus, and Fluorite for supporting clarity of thought and decision-making.

Aromatic herbs that align with Aquarius include Dill for enhancing protection and clarity in relationships, Lavender for calming the mind and fostering peace, Eucalyptus for cleansing and refreshing while promoting mental clarity, Sage for purification, Rosemary for boosting memory and intuition, Peppermint for invigorating the mind and sparking creativity, Basil for encouraging love and protection while enhancing clarity, and the dreamy Mugwort for supporting dream work and psychic abilities.

When it comes to essential oils, Aquarians will benefit from Neroli Oil, which is uplifting and calming, promoting emotional balance; Frankincense Oil, which enhances spiritual connection and meditation; and Patchouli Oil, which is grounding and balancing, encouraging self-expression. These elements resonate with the innovative, humanitarian, and often unconventional essence of Aquarius, making them perfect for spells or rituals connected to this zodiac sign.

Pisces: The Dreamer

Pisces, the final sign of the zodiac, is often referred to as "The Dreamer." Governed by the element of water and ruled by the expansive planet Neptune, those born under this sign are known for their intuition, creativity, and deep emotional currents. As a water sign, Pisces embodies the fluidity of feelings and the ethereal nature of dreams. They are natural empaths, often absorbing the emotions of others and channeling them through their rich imaginations. This sensitivity makes them adept at understanding the unseen forces that guide our lives, making them particularly skilled in both astrology and witchcraft.

For practitioners of astrology and witchcraft, tapping into the Piscean energy can enhance spellcasting and rituals. Pisces is associated with intuition and the subconscious, making it an ideal sign for spells aimed at enhancing dreams, enhancing psychic abilities, or facilitating emotional healing. Incorporating elements such as water, moonlight, and reflective surfaces can amplify the Piscean influence, allowing practitioners to create a sacred space that resonates with the sign's essence. Rituals conducted during the Pisces season, typically from February 19 to March 20, can be particularly potent for manifesting dreams and desires, as the energy of this sign encourages exploration of the inner self.

When considering divination techniques, the Piscean qualities lend themselves beautifully to methods that rely on intuition and emotional insight. Tarot readings, particularly those focused on the Moon or Water cards, can be enriched by the Piscean perspective. Scrying, using water or crystal balls, is another effective divinatory practice that aligns with the dreamy nature of Pisces. By using the energy of this sign, practitioners can delve deeper into their subconscious, uncovering hidden truths and gaining clarity on their paths. The key is to create a serene environment that fosters relaxation and openness to receive messages from the universe.

For those interested in manifestation rituals, the energy of Pisces can be particularly useful during significant astrological events like the New Moon or the Spring Equinox. During these times, practitioners can craft rituals that focus on setting intentions related to dreams, creativity, and emotional healing. Incorporating water elements—such as sea salt, ocean water, or herbal infusions—can enhance the ritual's effectiveness. Additionally, using crystals associated with Pisces, such as amethyst, aquamarine, or labradorite, can help amplify the energy of the ritual and foster a deeper connection to the Piscean archetype.

Pisces thrive in deep waters, and these stones resonate perfectly with their soulful nature. Amethyst serves as a calming crystal, enhancing intuition and spiritual awareness. Aquamarine is renowned for its soothing qualities, fostering peace and emotional healing. Fluorite clears the mind and sharpens focus, ideal for the dreamy essence of Pisces. Moonstone nurtures intuition and emotional balance, making it a perfect companion for their sensitivity. Lapis Lazuli encourages wisdom and self-awareness, promoting spiritual growth. Rose Quartz embodies love and compassion, facilitating emotional healing. Citrine attracts abundance and positivity, uplifting the Piscean spirit, while Sodalite supports rational thought and emotional harmony.

Herbs that resonate with Pisces include Lavender, known for its calming effects that help alleviate anxiety, and Dandelion, which is linked to wishes and dreams, aiding in manifesting intentions. Basil is useful for protection and purification, while Chamomile offers relaxation and emotional solace, often infused in teas or baths. Mugwort is associated with dreams and psychic abilities, making it beneficial for dream work. Jasmine promotes relaxation and emotional healing, frequently utilized in rituals, and Water Lily symbolizes purity and spiritual awakening, featured in various spells.

Essential oils also play a significant role for Pisces. Patchouli grounds energy and enhances meditation, while Ylang Ylang fosters emotional balance with its calming properties. Sandalwood is favored for meditation and spiritual practices, amplifying intuition. Rosemary is often incorporated into spells for clarity and protection, enhancing mental sharpness. And coconut water is utilized in cleansing rituals, providing emotional nourishment.

These elements can amplify the inherent intuitive and emotional traits of Pisces, making them ideal for diverse magical practices and rituals. Understanding the elemental connection of Pisces to water is crucial for those practicing elemental astrology. This relationship highlights the importance of fluidity and adaptability in both life and magical practices. Water is a purifying and transformative element, and including it into rituals can facilitate emotional release and renewal. By aligning with the elemental energies of Pisces, practitioners can create powerful spells and rituals that resonate with the dreamer's spirit, inviting creativity, intuition, and healing into their lives. As you explore the depths of Piscean energy, remember that dreams are not merely fantasies—they are the blueprints of our soul's desires, waiting to be manifested into reality.

Astrological Spellcasting

Crafting spells for each zodiac sign involves a deep understanding of the unique traits, energies, and elemental associations that define each astrological symbol. Every sign carries its own strengths and weaknesses, influencing the type of spells that can be effectively crafted and employed. By aligning your spellwork with the intrinsic characteristics of each zodiac sign, you can amplify your intentions and enhance the power of your rituals. This subchapter will guide you in tailoring spells that resonate with the specific attributes of each sign, allowing you to use their energies for personal growth and manifestation.

Aries, as the first sign of the zodiac, embodies the qualities of initiation, courage, and action. Spells crafted for Aries should focus on igniting passion and courage, making them ideal for rituals aimed at starting new ventures or overcoming obstacles. Incorporating fire elements, such as candles or incense, can enhance the potency of these spells. Conversely, Taurus, representing stability and sensuality, benefits from spells that promote abundance and security. Utilizing earth elements like herbs and crystals such as citrine can help ground the energy of the ritual while attracting prosperity and comfort.

Gemini, ruled by Mercury, thrives on communication and adaptability. Spells for this sign can center around enhancing clarity in communication or fostering creativity. Incorporating air elements, such as feathers or incense, can help elevate the energy and intention. In contrast, Cancer, governed by the moon, resonates with emotions and intuition. Spells for Cancer should focus on healing and nurturing, utilizing water elements like sea salt or moon water to enhance emotional balance and domestic harmony. Each sign's elemental association plays a crucial role in determining the most effective spell components and intentions.

As we journey through the zodiac, we find Leo, the sign of self-expression and leadership, which benefits from spells that amplify confidence and personal power. Fire elements, particularly vibrant colors and bold crystals like tiger's eye, can enhance these spells' effectiveness. Virgo, the analytical and meticulous sign, is best suited for spells that promote organization and health. Earth elements, such as grounding stones and herbal infusions, can help channel Virgo's energies towards productive outcomes. The relationship between each sign and its corresponding element is essential in crafting spells that resonate deeply with the practitioner's intentions.

When designing astrological rituals for manifestation, consider the timing of astrological events, such as eclipses or planetary transits, to further empower your spellwork. For instance, a full moon in Pisces can be an opportune time for spells related to intuition and emotional healing, while a new moon in Capricorn might be ideal for setting intentions related to career and structure. Additionally, integrating zodiac-based crystals and gemstones into your rituals can enhance the spell's efficacy. Each sign has specific stones that resonate with its energies, such as amethyst for Pisces and garnet for Aries. By thoughtfully combining these elements, practitioners can create powerful spells that use the celestial energies of their zodiac sign, leading to profound personal transformation and fulfillment.

Timing Spells with Astrological Events

Timing spells with astrological events is a profound practice that enhances the efficacy of your rituals by aligning them with the celestial movements that influence our lives. Each zodiac sign possesses unique traits and energies that can be used through tailored spells, making it essential to consider the timing of your practice in relation to astrological events. By understanding the cycles of the moon, the positions of the planets, and significant astrological phenomena, practitioners can maximize the potential for manifestation and divination, ensuring that their efforts resonate harmoniously with the cosmos.

The lunar cycle is one of the most vital aspects of astrological timing. The New Moon serves as a powerful time for setting intentions and beginning new projects, while the Full Moon is ideal for releasing negativity and completing endeavors. Each zodiac sign corresponds to specific lunar phases, amplifying the energy of spells. For instance, a New Moon in Taurus can be an auspicious time for spells related to financial stability and material abundance, while a Full Moon in Scorpio can facilitate deep emotional healing and transformation. Understanding these correlations allows practitioners to craft rituals that resonate deeply with the lunar energies, enhancing their effectiveness.

In addition to lunar phases, planetary transits also play a crucial role in spell timing. Each planet embodies distinct energies, and their movements through the zodiac can greatly influence the potency of spells. For example, Venus, the planet of love and beauty, is particularly powerful when transiting through Taurus or Libra, making it an ideal time for love spells or rituals aimed at enhancing personal beauty. Conversely, Mars, the planet of action and aggression, is best utilized for spells focused on courage and assertiveness when it moves through

Aries or Scorpio. By aligning spellwork with these planetary influences, practitioners can tap into the inherent power of the cosmos, amplifying their intentions.

Astrological events such as eclipses and retrogrades also provide unique opportunities for spellcasting. Eclipses are transformative times that can herald significant changes, making them ideal for spells focused on major life shifts, whether it be starting anew or letting go of the past. On the other hand, retrogrades, especially Mercury retrograde, are often regarded as times for reflection rather than action, making them suitable for introspective rituals and divination practices. Understanding the nuances of these events allows practitioners to navigate their spellcasting with greater awareness, ensuring that they are in harmony with the larger cosmic rhythms.

Lastly, elemental astrology is a crucial element in timing spells, as each zodiac sign is associated with one of the four elements: earth, air, fire, and water. By recognizing the elemental correspondences, practitioners can craft rituals that align with their specific zodiac influences. For instance, spells performed during a fire sign's season can use the energy of passion and creativity, while rituals in an earth sign's season can focus on stability and material growth. Additionally, including zodiac-based crystals and gemstones that resonate with the astrological energies at play can further amplify the effects of your spellwork. By thoughtfully timing your spells with astrological events and considering elemental influences, you deepen your connection to the universe and enhance your magical practice.

Enhancing Spells with Zodiac Traits

Enhancing spells with zodiac traits involves a deep understanding of the unique characteristics and energies associated with each astrological sign. By aligning spellwork with these traits, practitioners can amplify the effectiveness of their rituals. Each zodiac sign is governed by specific elements, ruling planets, and intrinsic qualities that influence how spells manifest. For instance, fire signs—Aries, Leo, and Sagittarius—embody passion and action, making them excellent candidates for spells focused on motivation and courage. Conversely, earth signs—Taurus, Virgo, and Capricorn—reflect stability and material concerns, which can enhance spells related to financial growth and practicality.

Astrological spellcasting requires a thoughtful approach to the traits of each sign. When crafting a spell, consider the sign's ruling planet and element. For example, a spell for emotional healing could incorporate the nurturing qualities of Cancer, combined with the intuitive powers of the Moon, its ruling celestial body. Incorporating the element of water—associated with fluidity and healing—can further enhance this spell, allowing for a deeper emotional release and renewal. Utilizing these astrological correlations not only strengthens the spell but also aligns the practitioner's intentions with the cosmic energies at play.

Divination practices can also benefit from zodiac traits. Techniques such as tarot readings or astrology chart interpretations can reveal insights based on the positions of celestial bodies within a zodiac framework. Practitioners can use their natal chart to identify strengths and weaknesses, tailoring their divination methods to explore questions pertinent to their astrological influences. For instance, a Leo might focus on creative pursuits during a reading, while a Capricorn could seek guidance on career choices. By aligning divination with zodiac energies, practitioners can achieve more personalized and relevant insights.

Astrological rituals for manifestation use specific celestial events to maximize spiritual and material goals. Events such as full moons, eclipses, and planetary transits play a crucial role in amplifying intentions. For example, a new moon in Virgo, known for its organizational and analytical traits, can be an ideal time to set intentions for personal development and health. By creating rituals that resonate with these astrological occurrences, practitioners can align their desires with the natural rhythms of the universe, leading to more effective manifestations.

The use of zodiac-based crystals and gemstones can further enhance the vibrational energy of spells. Each zodiac sign has specific stones that resonate with its characteristics. For instance, Taurus often connects with rose quartz for love and emotional healing, while Sagittarius might benefit from amethyst for spiritual growth and clarity. Incorporating these stones into spellwork—such as placing them on an altar or wearing them during rituals—can significantly amplify the energies being invoked. By understanding and utilizing these elements, practitioners can create a harmonious blend of astrology and witchcraft that elevates their spiritual practices.

Astrology for Divination

Astrological charts serve as the foundational blueprint for understanding the intricate dance of celestial bodies and their influence on our lives. At their core, these charts, also known as natal charts, map the positions of the planets, the Sun, and the Moon at the exact moment of an individual's birth. Each chart is unique, reflecting not only the cosmic configuration but also the energies and traits associated with the twelve zodiac signs. For those engaged in astrology and witchcraft, mastering the basics of astrological charts is essential. It enables a deeper connection to the universe and enhances the effectiveness of spells and rituals tailored to individual zodiac traits.

Beyond the basic interpretation, astrological charts can be utilized for spellcasting that aligns with the energies of specific zodiac signs. Each sign carries its own unique characteristics—Aries embodies courage and action, while Pisces resonates with intuition and creativity. By exploring these traits, practitioners can craft spells that tap into the inherent strengths of each sign. For instance, a spell aimed at fostering confidence might be particularly effective during the Aries season, while a manifestation ritual focused on emotional healing could align with the energies of Cancer. This harmonization of astrology and witchcraft not only enriches the spellcasting process but also amplifies the potential outcomes.

Astrological charts also play a pivotal role in divination practices. Techniques such as horary astrology, which answers specific questions based on the positions of planets at the time the question is posed, can provide profound insights into future events. Additionally, transits—where planets move through the zodiac signs—offer a dynamic lens through which practitioners can forecast personal and global shifts. By interpreting these astrological movements, individuals can gain clarity on opportunities and challenges ahead, allowing for informed decision-making and deeper spiritual alignment.

Rituals aligned with astrological events, such as eclipses or significant planetary transits, can significantly enhance personal goals and intentions. These celestial occurrences are believed to amplify energies, making them ideal times for manifestation. Practitioners can create rituals that use these potent moments, such as setting intentions under a new moon or releasing negativity during a full moon. By integrating astrological events into their spiritual practices, individuals can align their intentions with the natural rhythm of the universe, fostering a sense of empowerment and connection.

Lastly, elemental astrology offers a unique perspective that intertwines the four elements—earth, air, fire, and water—with the zodiac signs, enriching the practice of witchcraft. Each element corresponds to specific signs and carries distinct energies that can be utilized in magical workings. For example, earth signs like Taurus and Virgo resonate with grounding and stability, making them ideal for spells related to prosperity and security. In contrast, fire signs such as Leo and Sagittarius embody passion and creativity, lending themselves well to spells that require courage and inspiration. By including elemental energies into astrological practices, individuals can enhance their spellwork and deepen their connection to both the cosmos and the natural world.

Using Zodiac Signs in Tarot Reading

In the realm of tarot reading, the incorporation of zodiac signs adds a nuanced layer of interpretation that can deepen the understanding of a reading. Each zodiac sign is imbued with distinct characteristics, traits, and elemental influences, which can inform the way cards are perceived and their meanings interpreted. By aligning tarot spreads with the attributes of specific zodiac signs, practitioners can create readings that resonate more profoundly with the querent's personal energies and life situations. This harmonious integration not only enhances clarity but also enables a richer connection to the spiritual and astrological dimensions of the reading.

Astrology and tarot share a common foundation in symbolism and archetypes, making their combination particularly potent. Each zodiac sign corresponds to specific tarot cards, often linked through their elemental associations or the personalities that embody those signs. For instance, Aries is often connected with the Emperor card, symbolizing leadership and authority, while Pisces resonates with the Moon, representing intuition and dreams. By recognizing these connections, readers can tailor their interpretations based on the sign's inherent traits, providing a more personalized and relevant reading experience.

When engaging in astrological spellcasting, the synergy between zodiac signs and tarot can be further explored. Each sign possesses unique energies that can be used in spells designed to amplify specific intentions. For example, a spell for manifestation during a full moon in Taurus might incorporate the Hierophant card to invoke stability and groundedness. Understanding these intricate relationships allows practitioners to craft spells that not only align with the celestial influences at play but also resonate with the querent's personal zodiac characteristics, resulting in more effective outcomes.

Astrological rituals also benefit from the integration of tarot. By timing rituals to align with significant astrological events—such as the New Moon in Leo or a Mercury retrograde—practitioners can utilize tarot cards to identify themes and intentions. For instance, during a ritual focused on communication during Mercury retrograde, drawing the Eight of Wands can signify a need for clarity and swift action. These rituals become dynamic when informed by the qualities of the zodiac sign involved, allowing practitioners to set intentions that are in harmony with both the energies of the cosmos and their personal spiritual journeys.

The use of crystals and gemstones based on your zodiac sign can enhance tarot readings, serving as powerful allies in both divination and manifestation. Each zodiac sign is associated with specific stones that resonate with its energies—such as amethyst for Pisces or garnet for Aries. Incorporating these crystals into tarot spreads can amplify the reading's insights and help ground the querent in their intentions. By selecting crystals that correspond with their zodiac signs, individuals can create a sacred space that fosters clarity, focus, and alignment, ultimately enhancing their tarot experience and deepening their connection to the astrological influences at play.

Planetary Influences on Divination Techniques

Planetary influences play a significant role in the practices of divination and spellcasting, intertwining the cosmic energies of the celestial bodies with the personal vibrations of the zodiac signs. Each planet embodies unique characteristics and energies that can enhance or inhibit the effectiveness of various divination techniques. Understanding these planetary influences allows practitioners to align their rituals and spells with the natural rhythms of the universe, fostering a more profound connection between the practitioner and the cosmos.

The twelve zodiac signs each correspond to specific planetary rulers, which imbue them with distinct traits and energies. For instance, Mars, the planet of action and aggression, rules Aries and can amplify the assertiveness in spells focused on courage and determination. Conversely, Venus, the planet of love and beauty, governs Taurus and Libra, enriching rituals aimed at attraction and harmony. By recognizing the planetary rulers of each sign, practitioners can tailor their divination techniques to resonate with these energies, ensuring that their readings and predictions align with the cosmic influences at play.

Astrological charts serve as powerful tools for divination, revealing the positions of the planets and their aspects at any given time. These charts can guide practitioners in choosing auspicious times for specific rituals or spells, enhancing their efficacy. For example, conducting a divination session during a waxing moon, when the moon is growing, can provide insights into growth and expansion, while a reading during a waning moon may offer clarity on release and letting go. By integrating astrological timing into divination practices, practitioners can use the celestial energies to deepen their insights and predictions.

Astrological rituals for manifestation can also be significantly enhanced by understanding the influences of planetary transits and events. Eclipses, for example, are powerful celestial phenomena that signify change and transformation. A ritual performed during a lunar eclipse can be particularly potent for releasing old patterns, while a solar eclipse can be an ideal time for setting new intentions. By aligning their practices with these astronomical events, practitioners can tap into the heightened energies available during these times, allowing for more profound and impactful manifestations.

Elemental astrology further enriches the understanding of planetary influences on divination techniques. Each zodiac sign is associated with one of the four elements—earth, air, fire, or water—each carrying its own unique energy that can be invoked during rituals. For instance, fire signs such as Leo and

Sagittarius resonate with passion and creativity, making them ideal for spells aimed at inspiration and motivation. Meanwhile, water signs like Cancer and Pisces are connected to emotions and intuition, enhancing divination practices that require sensitivity and insight. By recognizing the elemental connections of their zodiac signs, practitioners can choose appropriate crystals and gemstones that amplify their intentions, creating a holistic approach to their astrological and magical practices.

Astrology and Runes

Astrology and runes are two ancient systems of divination that, while distinct in their origins and methodologies, share a profound connection in their ability to provide insight and guidance. For practitioners of astrology and witchcraft, the combination of these two practices can deepen one's understanding of the cosmos and enhance magical workings. Runes, with their rich historical significance in Norse and Celtic traditions, complement astrological practices by offering symbolic meanings that can be used during spells, rituals, and divination. This synergy allows individuals to tap into the energies of both the celestial bodies and the earth, creating a holistic approach to personal empowerment and spiritual growth.

In the realm of astrological spellcasting, each zodiac sign embodies unique traits and energies that can be magnified through using runes. By aligning specific runes with the characteristics of each sign, practitioners can create more potent spells tailored to their individual needs and desires. For example, the rune Fehu, representing wealth and abundance, can be used in conjunction with the Taurus energy to attract prosperity. Similarly, the rune Gebo, which signifies partnership and balance, can enhance love spells for Libra, fostering harmonious connections. This melding of astrological insight and runic symbolism not only enriches the spellcasting process but also empowers practitioners to manifest their intentions more effectively.

Astrology also serves as a powerful tool for divination, and the inclusion of runes can further enhance predictive techniques. By casting runes in conjunction with astrological charts, practitioners can gain a multi-dimensional understanding of their current circumstances and future possibilities. For instance, interpreting the placement of planets alongside rune spreads can provide clarity on how celestial events influence personal situations. This technique invites a deeper exploration of the interconnectedness of cosmic energies and personal destiny, allowing individuals to navigate their paths with greater awareness and intention.

Rituals designed around astrological events, such

as eclipses or planetary transits, can also benefit from the incorporation of runes. These moments in time are powerful catalysts for change and manifestation, and by embedding runic symbols into these rituals, practitioners can amplify their intentions. For example, during a lunar eclipse, one might use the rune Wunjo, symbolizing joy and success, to manifest positive outcomes. The combination of the transformative energies of the astrological event with the focused intention of the runic symbols creates a dynamic ritual space where personal goals can be realized.

Elemental astrology further enhances the interplay between astrology and runes, as each zodiac sign is associated with one of the four elements: earth, air, fire, or water. Understanding these elemental correspondences allows practitioners to select runes that resonate with the elemental energies of their zodiac sign. For example, an air sign like Gemini might benefit from the rune Laguz, which relates to intuition and flow, while a fire sign like Aries may find empowerment through the rune Tiwaz, symbolizing courage and victory. By consciously aligning elemental influences with astrological and runic practices, individuals can deepen their spiritual journeys and cultivate a more profound connection to the universe.

Astrological Rituals for Manifestation

Aligning rituals with lunar phases is a time-honored practice that enhances the potency of spells and intentions. The moon's cyclical journey through its phases—new, waxing, full, and waning—provides a natural rhythm that can be used to align personal energies with the cosmos. Each phase carries unique energies that can be tapped into for various purposes, making it essential for practitioners of astrology and witchcraft to understand how to synchronize their rituals with these lunar cycles. By doing so, one can amplify the effectiveness of their intentions and deepen their connection with the universe.

The new moon, symbolizing new beginnings and potential, is an ideal time for setting intentions and initiating new projects. This phase is characterized by darkness, representing a blank slate where possibilities abound. Rituals performed during the new moon should focus on manifestation and goal-setting, allowing practitioners to plant the seeds of their desires. Incorporating elements that resonate with the specific zodiac sign in the new moon's phase can further enhance the ritual's effectiveness. For instance, a new moon in Aries may call for bold intentions and a focus on self-empowerment, while a new moon in Pisces emphasizes creativity and spiritual growth.

As the moon waxes, its light increases, symbolizing growth and expansion. This phase is perfect for rituals that require nurturing and development of intentions set during the new moon. Practitioners can use this energy by including spells that promote abundance, success, and personal growth. During the waxing phase, focusing on the elements associated with one's zodiac sign can enhance the ritual's effectiveness. For example, an Earth sign might incorporate grounding crystals or herbs, while a Fire sign could use candles to invoke passion and motivation. This alignment not only amplifies the energy of the ritual but also creates a deeper connection to the elemental forces at play.

The full moon is a time of culmination, illumination, and heightened energy. It is the peak of the lunar cycle, making it the best time for rituals involving release, gratitude, and reflection. Practitioners can use this phase to celebrate accomplishments and acknowledge what no longer serves them. Divination practices are particularly potent during the full moon, allowing for heightened intuition and insight. Incorporating zodiac-specific items, such as crystals or symbols, can amplify the energy of the full moon ritual. For instance, a full moon in Scorpio may invite deep emotional exploration and transformation, while a full moon in Gemini encourages communication and sharing of ideas.

The waning moon represents a time of letting go and introspection. This phase is ideal for rituals focused on release, healing, and clearing away negativity. Practitioners can use this time to break habits or release burdens that hinder personal growth. Aligning these release rituals with the elemental associations of their zodiac signs can enhance their efficacy. For example, Water signs may benefit from cleansing rituals involving water, while Air signs might focus on mental clarity and releasing limiting beliefs. By understanding and aligning rituals with the lunar phases, practitioners can create a powerful synergy between their intentions and the celestial energies, fostering a deeper, more harmonious relationship with the universe.

Using Eclipse Energy for Transformation

Eclipses have long been seen as powerful celestial events, embodying the duality of endings and beginnings. In the realm of astrology and witchcraft, these phenomena serve as potent catalysts for transformation, allowing practitioners to tap into the cosmic energies for personal growth and manifestation. By understanding the significance of eclipses, individuals can use their unique vibrations to facilitate change, release old patterns, and invite new opportunities into their lives. This subchapter explores the profound implications of eclipses, emphasizing how they can be utilized for transformative rituals and spells.

Astrologically, eclipses occur when the Sun, Moon, and Earth align in a way that obscures one celestial body from another. Solar eclipses symbolize new beginnings and fresh starts, while lunar eclipses often signify closure and the culmination of cycles. Each zodiac sign experiences these eclipses differently, depending on where they fall in one's astrological chart. By analyzing the specific house and aspects involved, practitioners can gain insight into which areas of life are ripe for transformation, allowing them to tailor their rituals and spells accordingly. This astrological awareness empowers individuals to make the most of these potent lunar events.

To effectively utilize the energies of eclipses, practitioners can engage in targeted rituals that align with their zodiac sign and personal goals. For instance, during a solar eclipse, an Aries might focus on initiating bold changes in their career, while a Cancer may channel their energies toward nurturing personal relationships. Utilizing tools such as candles, herbs, and crystals that resonate with their zodiac traits can amplify the effects of these rituals. For instance, an Aries can incorporate garnet for passion and motivation, while a Cancer might choose moonstone for intuition and emotional healing. By aligning their intentions with the energies of their sign during eclipses, individuals can create a powerful synergy that enhances their transformative journey.

Eclipses also serve as a time for divination, offering unique insights into future possibilities. Practitioners can utilize astrological charts to interpret the significance of the eclipse in relation to their personal circumstances. Techniques such as scrying, tarot reading, or pendulum work can be particularly effective during this time, as the heightened energy allows for clearer connections to the spiritual realm. By asking specific questions related to the areas of life affected by the eclipse, individuals can receive guidance that aids their transformation process. This divination aspect not only enriches the practice but also deepens the understanding of one's life path and the unfolding journey.

The elemental associations of zodiac signs can enhance the effectiveness of eclipse rituals. Each sign corresponds to one of the four elements—earth, air, fire, or water—each carrying distinct energies and characteristics. For example, a Virgo, an earth sign, may benefit from grounding rituals that involve soil or stones, while a Leo, a fire sign, may use the transformative energy of flames during their rituals.

By integrating elemental practices with the energies of an eclipse, practitioners can create a more holistic approach to transformation, aligning their physical, emotional, and spiritual selves. This synergy not only strengthens their connection to the cosmos but also empowers them to manifest their desires more concretely.

In conclusion, eclipses are profound opportunities for transformation in the astrological and witchcraft communities. By understanding their significance and aligning rituals with zodiac energies, practitioners can effectively use these celestial events for personal growth. Through targeted spellcasting, divination, and elemental practices, individuals can navigate the cycles of endings and beginnings, ultimately fostering a deeper connection to themselves and the universe. Embracing the power of eclipses opens pathways to profound change, allowing for the manifestation of one's true potential.

Planetary Transits and Their Energies

Planetary transits play a crucial role in astrology, influencing the energies and dynamics of our lives. Each transit corresponds to the movement of planets through the zodiac signs and their relationships with one another. These movements can create unique opportunities for growth, transformation, and manifestation. Understanding the energies associated with various planetary transits allows practitioners of astrology and witchcraft to use these celestial events to enhance their rituals, spells, and personal development. This subchapter delves into the significance of planetary transits, offering insight into how they can be effectively utilized for astrological spellcasting and manifestation.

One of the most important aspects of planetary transits is their ability to trigger specific energies that resonate with different zodiac signs. For instance, when Jupiter, the planet of expansion and abundance, transits through a sign, it can amplify the traits associated with that sign, making it an ideal time for spells focused on growth and prosperity. Conversely, transits of Saturn may bring challenges that require discipline and responsibility, presenting opportunities for practitioners to engage in rituals that promote resilience and inner strength. By aligning practices with these astrological movements, individuals can create a powerful synergy between their intentions and the energies present in the cosmos.

Astrological spellcasting benefits significantly from an understanding of planetary transits. By casting spells during particular transits, practitioners can enhance their effectiveness. For example, a spell for love and relationships may be most potent during a Venus transit, while a spell for career advancement aligns best with a Mercury transit. Such timing not only maximizes the likelihood of success but also deepens the connection between the caster and the astrological influences at play. This approach invites a harmonious interaction with the universe, allowing individuals to manifest their desires with greater clarity and purpose.

In addition to spellcasting, planetary transits can be employed in ritual practices designed for manifestation. Significant transits, such as eclipses or retrogrades, provide unique opportunities for introspection and transformation. Rituals performed during these times can help individuals release old patterns and invite new energies into their lives. For instance, a lunar eclipse may be a powerful moment for cleansing rituals, while a solar eclipse can serve as a catalyst for setting bold intentions. By aligning rituals with these celestial events, practitioners can use the heightened energies of the transits to support their personal goals and spiritual journeys.

Understanding the elemental associations of each zodiac sign can further enrich the practice of working with planetary transits. Each sign is linked to one of the four elements: earth, air, fire, or water, each carrying distinct energies and attributes. When a planet transits through a sign, its elemental influence can enhance the overall energy of the transit. For example, a fire sign transit may inspire courage and creativity, while a water sign transit may facilitate emotional healing and intuition. By including elemental correspondences into their practices, practitioners can deepen their connection to the energies of the zodiac and the cosmos, creating a more holistic approach to astrology and witchcraft.

Planetary transits are a fundamental aspect of astrological practice, providing a rich tapestry of energies that can be used for spellcasting, rituals, and personal growth. By understanding the nature of these transits and their influence on the zodiac signs, practitioners can create intentional practices that resonate with the rhythms of the cosmos. This not only enhances the potency of their magical work but also fosters a deeper connection to the universe and their spiritual path. As individuals engage with these celestial energies, they open themselves to transformative experiences that align with their highest aspirations.

Creating Personal Rituals for Goal Setting

Creating personal rituals for goal setting is a powerful way to align your intentions with the energies of the cosmos. By integrating astrology into your ritual practice, you can enhance your manifestation efforts, tapping into the celestial influences that correspond to your unique zodiac sign. This subchapter will guide you through the process of designing meaningful rituals that resonate with your astrological identity, allowing you to use the full potential of your goals.

It's essential to understand your zodiac sign's traits and elemental associations. Each sign embodies specific characteristics, strengths, and weaknesses that can inform your approach to goal setting. For instance, fire signs like Aries, Leo, and Sagittarius are naturally ambitious and driven, making them well-suited for bold and dynamic rituals. In contrast, earth signs such as Taurus, Virgo, and Capricorn may prefer grounded and practical approaches. By recognizing these attributes, you can craft rituals that not only feel authentic to you but also enhance your inherent strengths in pursuing your goals.

Incorporating astrological events into your rituals can further amplify your intentions. For example, the new moon is a potent time for setting intentions, while full moons are ideal for releasing what no longer serves you. By aligning your goal-setting rituals with these lunar phases, you create a synergy that enhances your manifestation efforts. Additionally, pay attention to significant planetary transits, such as retrogrades or conjunctions, which can impact your energy and focus. Timing your rituals around these celestial events can provide a supportive backdrop for your aspirations.

Utilizing zodiac-based crystals and gemstones can also elevate your ritual practice. Each sign is associated with specific stones that resonate with its energies, offering both magical and healing properties. For example, amethyst is often linked to Pisces for its intuitive qualities, while citrine is favored by Leos for its manifestation power. By including these crystals into your rituals—whether through meditation, placing them on your altar, or carrying them with you—you can enhance your connection to your goals and invite supportive energies into your life.

Personal rituals are highly individualized. While it's beneficial to draw inspiration from astrological insights, allow your intuition to guide you in crafting rituals that feel meaningful. Consider including elements such as visualization, affirmations, or even creative expressions like journaling or art. The key is to create a ritual that resonates with your soul and aligns with your aspirations. By merging your personal goals with the wisdom of astrology, you can create a powerful practice that supports your journey toward fulfillment and manifestation.

Elemental Astrology

The four elements—earth, air, fire, and water—are foundational to both astrology and witchcraft, forming a critical framework that informs the practices and beliefs of many spiritual traditions. Each element embodies distinct characteristics, energies, and qualities that correspond with specific zodiac signs, influencing personality traits, behaviors, and even the effectiveness of rituals. Understanding these elemental associations can enhance one's astrological practice, allowing practitioners to deepen their connection with the cosmos and use the power of these elements in spellcasting and ritual work.

Earth, the element of stability and practicality, is associated with the zodiac signs Taurus, Virgo, and Capricorn. Those governed by earth tend to be grounded, reliable, and focused on the material world. In witchcraft, earth is often invoked in rituals aimed at manifesting stability, abundance, and physical well-being. Crystals such as emeralds, onyx, and garnets resonate with earth energies, providing grounding and protection while amplifying the intentions set during spells. When creating rituals for earth signs, it is essential to incorporate elements of nature—such as soil, stones, or plants—to fully align with the earth's nurturing qualities.

Air represents intellect, communication, and the realm of ideas, linking it to the zodiac signs Gemini, Libra, and Aquarius. Those influenced by air are often seen as adaptable, social, and curious. In astrological spellcasting, air can be used to enhance clarity of thought, facilitate communication, and inspire creativity. Incorporating air-focused tools like feathers, incense, or sage can elevate rituals, inviting the energies of the winds to carry intentions and manifest desires. Crystals such as aquamarine and citrine are particularly effective for air signs, aiding in mental clarity and uplifting one's spirit, making them ideal companions for air-themed spells.

The element of fire embodies passion, transformation, and energy, connecting with the signs Aries, Leo, and Sagittarius. Fire signs are typically known for their enthusiasm, assertiveness, and a desire for action. In witchcraft, fire is used to ignite change, inspire courage, and fuel motivation. Candles, bonfires, or even the act of burning herbs during rituals can channel fire's vibrant energy. Crystals like carnelian and ruby resonate with this element, empowering spellwork that seeks to enhance personal power and courage. When crafting rituals for fire signs, it's beneficial to incorporate movements that evoke the dynamic nature of fire, such as dance or vocal expressions.

Water, the element of emotion, intuition, and healing, corresponds with the zodiac signs Cancer, Scorpio, and Pisces. Water signs are often empathetic, sensitive, and deeply connected to their feelings. In astrological rituals, water is utilized for emotional healing, intuition enhancement, and spiritual cleansing. Sacred waters, seashells, or representations of the moon can be included in rituals to invoke water's calming and restorative properties. Crystals like moonstone and labradorite are effective for water signs, amplifying intuition and emotional balance. Rituals for water signs often involve meditation or divination practices, allowing practitioners to tap into the flow of their emotions and inner wisdom.

By understanding the significance of the four elements in conjunction with astrological practices, practitioners can create powerful rituals and spells that resonate with their individual energies and intentions. Each element not only enriches the practice of witchcraft but also enhances the connection with the astrological framework that governs our lives. Whether seeking stability, inspiration, transformation, or healing, embracing the elemental energies allows for a more profound exploration of one's spiritual path, making the journey through astrology and witchcraft even more impactful and fulfilling.

Earth Signs - Grounding and Practical

Earth signs—Taurus, Virgo, and Capricorn—are the embodiment of stability, practicality, and groundedness. These signs are deeply connected to the physical realm, making them particularly attuned to rituals and spells that focus on material manifestations and earthly energies. For those engaged in astrology and witchcraft, understanding the unique characteristics of Earth signs can significantly enhance the effectiveness of rituals and spellcasting. Grounding rituals serve to use the inherent strength of Earth energy, allowing practitioners to connect with the natural world and their own physicality, thereby facilitating a deeper sense of stability and security in their lives.

One effective grounding ritual involves creating a sacred space filled with Earth elements, such as soil, stones, and plants. Begin by selecting a quiet area in your home or outdoors where you feel relaxed and undisturbed. Arrange your chosen elements in a circle, and place a clear quartz crystal at the center to amplify the energy of your intentions. As you sit within this circle, close your eyes and take several deep breaths, visualizing roots extending from your body into the Earth. This visualization helps to stabilize your energy and foster a sense of connection with the ground beneath you, promoting feelings of safety and calm—qualities that resonate deeply with

Earth signs.

In addition to grounding rituals, Earth signs can benefit from specific spells that capitalize on their natural traits. For instance, a spell for abundance may involve creating a small altar featuring symbols of prosperity, such as coins, green candles, and a bowl of salt—representing Earth's wealth. As you light the candles, recite affirmations that align with your intentions for abundance. The combination of focused intention and the Earth elements will amplify the spell's effectiveness, helping to manifest your desires in the material world. This approach not only honors the Earth signs' affinity for practical outcomes but also reinforces their connection to the physical aspects of life.

Astrological events and planetary transits offer powerful opportunities for Earth signs to engage in manifestation rituals. For example, during a New Moon in an Earth sign, practitioners can set intentions related to career advancement, financial stability, or personal growth. Writing these intentions on a piece of paper and burying it in the Earth or planting it alongside a seed can symbolize the nurturing of your goals. As the seed grows, so too will your intentions, making this a fitting ritual for Earth signs who thrive on tangible results. This practice emphasizes the importance of aligning personal aspirations with the rhythms of the universe, enhancing the likelihood of achieving one's goals.

To further enhance their magical practices, Earth signs can incorporate specific crystals and gemstones that resonate with their energy. Crystals such as green aventurine for prosperity, smoky quartz for grounding, and carnelian for motivation are particularly beneficial for Earth sign practitioners. These stones can be used in rituals or kept in one's personal space to amplify the desired energies. By aligning their spellcasting with the elemental properties of Earth and the unique characteristics of their zodiac signs, practitioners can create a harmonious balance between their intentions and the natural world, deepening their spiritual practice while honoring the practicality that Earth signs represent.

Air Signs - Intellectual and Communicative

Air signs, comprising Gemini, Libra, and Aquarius, are characterized by their intellectual curiosity and communicative prowess. These signs are often associated with the mental realm, and their energy reflects an innate ability to think critically, engage in lively discussions, and connect with others on a cerebral level. In the context of astrology and witchcraft, understanding the unique traits of air signs can enhance your spellcasting practices, divination techniques, and ritual work, allowing you to use the distinctive energies that these signs embody.

To begin with, the intellectual nature of air signs provides a fertile ground for astrological spellcasting. When crafting spells that align with the qualities of these signs, consider focusing on themes of communication, knowledge, and social connections. For instance, a spell designed to enhance clarity in communication can be particularly powerful during a Gemini moon phase or when Mercury, the planet of communication, is strong. Incorporating elements such as air incense, feathers, or even written affirmations can amplify the effectiveness of your intention, invoking the airy qualities that inspire clarity and insight.

In terms of divination, air signs excel in analytical thinking and abstract reasoning, making them ideal for techniques that require interpretation and intuition. Tarot readings, runes, or even astrology charts can be enhanced with the airy mindset that Gemini, Libra, and Aquarius provide. For those interested in predictive astrology, consider casting your charts during air sign seasons to tap into the heightened intellectual energy. This alignment can sharpen your ability to read the signs and symbols present in your divination practices, aiding in uncovering deeper insights and guidance.

Rituals for manifestation can also benefit from the influence of air signs, particularly when seeking to cultivate ideas and inspiration. During significant astrological events, such as eclipses or the ingress of a planet into an air sign, set aside time for rituals focused on brainstorming and creative expression. Use tools like vision boards, journaling, or group brainstorming sessions to channel the airy energy into tangible goals. The key to these rituals is to create a light and open atmosphere, allowing the flow of ideas to manifest effortlessly while inviting the winds of change to guide your intentions.

Finally, when considering the relationship between air signs and crystals, certain gems resonate deeply with their elemental nature. Crystals like aquamarine, blue lace agate, and clear quartz can enhance communication skills and intellectual clarity. Incorporating these stones into your spellwork or ritual practices can further amplify the effects of your intentions. For example, carrying a piece of blue lace agate during a presentation or discussion can help articulate thoughts more clearly, while meditating with aquamarine can open the mind to new ideas and perspectives. By recognizing and using the powers of air signs, you can enhance your astrological practices, creating a harmonious blend of intellect, communication, and manifestation in your spiritual journey.

Fire Signs - Passionate and Dynamic

Fire signs—Aries, Leo, and Sagittarius—embody the essence of dynamism and passion. Each of these zodiac signs is imbued with an elemental energy that fuels their natural inclination toward vibrant rituals and spellwork. The fire element represents creativity, enthusiasm, and a boldness that can ignite change and transformation. In the context of rituals, fire signs thrive on activities that reflect their spirited nature. They are drawn to rituals that stimulate their passions, helping them to use their inner fire for manifesting desires and achieving personal goals.

When creating rituals for fire signs, it is essential to incorporate elements that resonate with their fiery disposition. The use of candles, especially in vibrant colors like red, orange, and gold, can amplify the energy of these rituals. Lighting candles during a ritual not only symbolizes the fire element but also represents the illumination of the spirit and the will to act. Fire signs can engage in ritual practices that include dynamic movements, such as dancing or drumming, to channel their energy effectively. These activities help to cultivate an atmosphere of excitement and empowerment, enabling fire signs to connect deeply with their intentions and desires.

In addition to traditional rituals, fire signs can benefit from astrological spellcasting that aligns with their unique traits. For instance, Aries, known for its pioneering spirit, may find success in spells that focus on new beginnings and courage. Leo, with its natural flair for the dramatic, can channel its charisma into rituals aimed at self-expression and leadership. Sagittarius, the seeker of truth, may thrive in rituals that encourage exploration and adventure, whether that's through travel or intellectual pursuits. Tailoring these spells to the specific fire sign not only enhances their effectiveness but also engages the practitioner's innate qualities, making the process deeply personal and transformative.

Astrological events such as eclipses and planetary transits can serve as powerful catalysts for fire sign rituals. During a new moon, for example, fire signs can set intentions that align with their aspirations, using the energy of rebirth and new beginnings. Conversely, during a full moon, they may focus on releasing what no longer serves them, allowing space for new opportunities. Incorporating astrological insights into ritual practice enables fire signs to align their actions with the natural rhythms of the universe, enhancing the potential for manifestation and success.

Finally, the incorporation of zodiac-based crystals can further empower fire sign rituals. Crystals like carnelian, citrine, and ruby resonate strongly with the energies of Aries, Leo, and Sagittarius, respectively. These stones can be used during rituals, worn as talismans, or placed on altars to amplify the intentions set forth. By integrating these elements into their practices, fire signs can deepen their connection to the elemental forces at play, cultivating an environment that supports their passionate and dynamic natures. In doing so, they not only honor their astrological heritage but also enhance their journey in the realms of witchcraft and spirituality.

Water Signs - Intuitive and Emotional

Water signs—Cancer, Scorpio, and Pisces—are known for their deep emotional intelligence and intuitive abilities. These signs are often described as the most sensitive of the zodiac, possessing an innate connection to the emotional currents that run through both themselves and others. This subchapter will explore how the qualities of water signs can be used in astrological spellcasting, divination, and rituals, emphasizing their unique ability to navigate the depths of human experience while also connecting with the spiritual realm.

At the heart of the water signs lies an extraordinary capacity for empathy and understanding. Cancers, with their nurturing nature, often serve as the caretakers of the zodiac, creating safe spaces for emotional expression. Scorpios, known for their intensity, dive into the depths of feelings that others may shy away from, revealing hidden truths and facilitating transformation. Meanwhile, Pisces embodies the dreamer, bringing a sense of compassion and connection to the collective unconscious. Understanding these emotional landscapes allows practitioners to craft spells and rituals that resonate with the watery essence of these signs, channeling their energies to foster healing, protection, and enlightenment.

In the realm of astrological divination, water signs are particularly adept at interpreting subtle signs from the universe. Utilizing techniques such as tarot reading or scrying with water, practitioners can tap into the intuitive knowledge that water signs embody. The fluidity of water allows for a dynamic approach to divination, where the practitioner can read the emotional undertones of situations and discern deeper meanings from the symbols presented. This intuitive insight is invaluable for those seeking clarity and guidance in their lives, especially during tumultuous times when emotions may cloud judgment.

Rituals for manifestation can be greatly enhanced by aligning with the energies of the water signs. The lunar phases, particularly the new moon and full moon, hold significant power for water signs, serving as potent times for emotional release and intention-setting. Crafting rituals that incorporate water elements—such as using saltwater for purification or including moonwater for intention-setting—can amplify the energies of the water signs. These rituals not only honor the emotional depth of the water signs but also allow practitioners to manifest their desires in alignment with their innermost feelings and intuition.

Finally, the connection between water signs and specific crystals is a vital aspect of their magical practices. Crystals such as aquamarine, moonstone, and labradorite resonate deeply with the emotional and intuitive qualities of water signs. These stones can be used in meditation, spellwork, and healing practices to enhance one's emotional clarity and spiritual connection. By including these zodiac-based crystals into their rituals, practitioners can align themselves more closely with the powerful energies of the water signs, fostering an environment of healing, intuition, and emotional well-being. Embracing the traits of water signs invites a richer understanding of the self and the world, paving the way for profound spiritual growth and connection.

Crystals and Gemstones for Each Zodiac Sign

The intersection of crystals and astrology presents a profound opportunity for those engaged in both practices to enhance their spiritual journeys. Crystals, with their unique vibrational energies, can amplify the qualities of specific zodiac signs, making them powerful allies in rituals and spellcasting. Each zodiac sign is associated with particular elemental energies—earth, air, fire, and water—that govern not only personality traits but also the types of crystals that resonate most harmoniously with them. By understanding how these elements interact with astrological influences, practitioners can use the power of crystals to enhance their manifestations, divinations, and rituals.

Astrological spellcasting benefits immensely from the incorporation of crystals tailored to each sign's inherent characteristics. For instance, Aries, a fire sign known for its boldness and energetic spirit, can benefit from using garnet or carnelian, which can enhance motivation and courage. On the other hand, Cancer, a water sign deeply connected to emotions, may find solace and balance through the nurturing energy of moonstone or rose quartz. Each crystal not only resonates with the sign's elemental energy but also amplifies its strengths, helping practitioners to channel their intentions effectively during spellwork.

Moreover, astrology serves as a powerful tool for divination, and crystals can enhance these practices. By aligning specific crystals with astrological charts, practitioners can gain deeper insights into their readings. For example, clear quartz can be used in conjunction with a natal chart to facilitate clarity and amplify intuitive insights during a tarot reading or astrological forecast. The vibrational frequencies of crystals can help to clear mental clutter, allowing for a more profound connection to the cosmos and the messages that arise within astrological alignments.

Rituals designed around astrological events, such as eclipses or planetary transits, also greatly benefit from the inclusion of crystals. These cosmic occurrences provide potent opportunities for manifestation, and the right crystals can enhance the energy of these rituals. During a full moon in Leo, for instance, using citrine can help participants tap into their creativity and self-expression, while during a new moon in Virgo, the grounding properties of jasper can assist in setting intentions related to health and organization. By strategically choosing crystals that resonate with the energies at play, practitioners can create rituals that are not only meaningful but also highly effective.

Lastly, an understanding of elemental astrology further enriches the practice of integrating crystals. Each element corresponds to specific zodiac signs and, by extension, particular crystals. Earth signs like Taurus and Capricorn resonate with stones such as emerald and onyx, which promote stability and grounding. Air signs, including Gemini and Libra, may find that crystals like aquamarine and fluorite enhance communication and mental clarity. By recognizing the elemental relationships at play, practitioners can craft a more holistic approach to their astrological and crystal practices, creating a powerful synergy that supports their spiritual growth and personal goals.

Selecting Crystals for Each Zodiac Sign

Selecting crystals for each zodiac sign is not merely a matter of preference; it is an intricate practice that intertwines the energies of both the celestial and earthly realms. Each zodiac sign possesses unique traits, strengths, and weaknesses, which can be harmonized and amplified by the right crystals. Understanding the elemental associations and astrological characteristics of each sign allows practitioners to select crystals that resonate deeply with their intrinsic nature. This careful selection process enhances spellcasting, divination, and rituals, creating a profound synergy between a person's astrological identity and their chosen stones.

Aries, for instance, is a fire sign characterized by passion, courage, and a pioneering spirit. Crystals such as garnet and carnelian can be particularly beneficial for Aries individuals, as they promote motivation and vitality. Garnet aids in grounding the fiery energy of Aries, ensuring that their ambition doesn't lead to recklessness. On the other hand, carnelian stimulates creativity and encourages action, aligning perfectly with the assertive nature of this sign. Incorporating these stones into rituals can enhance their effectiveness, making the energy of Aries even more potent during astrological events like the new moon or spring equinox.

Taurus, an earth sign, thrives on stability, sensuality, and practicality. Crystals like rose quartz and emerald resonate well with Taurus individuals, helping them cultivate love and abundance. Rose quartz can deepen emotional connections, while emerald is known for its ability to attract wealth and prosperity. For Taureans, selecting crystals that enhance their natural tendencies toward nurturing and security can significantly amplify their intentions during rituals focused on manifestation or during significant planetary transits, such as Venus retrograde, which influences love and relationships.

Gemini, an air sign known for its duality and adaptability, benefits from crystals such as aquamarine and citrine. Aquamarine, with its calming energy, helps Gemini navigate their sometimes tumultuous thoughts and emotions, fostering clarity and communication. Citrine, often referred to as the "merchant's stone," enhances creativity and personal power, making it ideal for Geminis looking to manifest their ideas into reality. When engaging in divinatory practices, these crystals can ground the scattered energies of Gemini, allowing for sharper insights and more accurate readings during astrological alignments.

The elemental connections of each zodiac sign further enhance the practice of crystal selection. Fire signs, like Leo and Sagittarius, thrive on crystals that invigorate and inspire, such as sunstone and tiger's eye. Water signs, including Cancer and Pisces, benefit from stones that enhance intuition and emotional depth, such as moonstone and labradorite. Earth signs, like Virgo and Capricorn, resonate with grounding and practical stones like hematite and black tourmaline, while air signs often seek clarity and communication through crystals like clear quartz and sodalite. By aligning crystal choices with elemental and astrological traits, practitioners can create a powerful toolkit for their spiritual practices, deepening their connection to the universe and enhancing their personal growth.

Methods of Using Crystals in Spells and Rituals

Crystals have long been revered for their energetic properties and are a powerful tool in the practice of spells and rituals within the realms of astrology and witchcraft. Each zodiac sign corresponds to specific crystals that resonate with its unique traits and energies, making them effective allies in spellcasting and ritual work. Understanding the methods of using crystals can enhance your spiritual practices, allowing you to tap into the cosmic forces that govern our lives. This subchapter explores various methods for including crystals into your astrological rituals and spells, providing you with practical guidance to deepen your connection with both the Earth and the cosmos.

One fundamental approach is to select crystals that align with your zodiac sign or the astrological event you are working with. For instance, a Leo may choose sunstone or citrine to use the fiery energy of their sign, while a Pisces might find solace in aquamarine or amethyst, which resonate with their water element. Incorporating these stones into your rituals can amplify the intentions set forth in your spell. To do this, hold the chosen crystal in your hand while visualizing your desired outcome, allowing the crystal's energy to merge with your intention. This method not only enhances focus but also creates a powerful energetic circuit that draws on the vibrational attributes of both the crystal and your astrological alignment.

Another effective technique involves creating crystal grids, which are geometric arrangements of crystals designed to amplify energy for specific purposes. When crafting a grid, consider the elemental attributes of your zodiac sign. For example, an Earth sign like Taurus might use a grid featuring grounding stones such as hematite or green aventurine, while a Fire sign like Aries could incorporate energetic stones like garnet or red jasper. Place the central crystal at the heart of the grid, representing your core intention, and surround it with complementary stones that resonate with your goal. Activating the grid through meditation or focused intention can enhance the manifestations of your spell, particularly during auspicious astrological events like full moons or eclipses.

Astrological rituals can also benefit from the incorporation of crystals during specific planetary transits or alignments. For instance, during a Mercury retrograde, using stones such as labradorite or clear quartz can help facilitate clear communication and protect against misunderstandings. By creating a dedicated space with these crystals, you can establish a sacred environment for your ritual. Lighting candles, burning incense, or using essential oils that correspond to your zodiac sign can further enhance the energy as you focus on your intentions. This synergy of elements, combined with the power of crystals, can lead to profound insights and manifestations aligned with the cosmic energies at play.

Consider utilizing crystals for divination purposes. By including them into your astrological chart readings or using them alongside tarot cards, you can gain deeper insights into your path. For instance, drawing a crystal card from your collection while interpreting a tarot spread can provide clarity and confirmation of insights drawn from the cards. Each crystal can serve as a symbolic representation of the energies at play in your astrological chart, helping to illuminate areas where you may need to focus your energy or make adjustments. This method not only enriches your divination practice but also reinforces the connection between astrology and crystal work.

The energy of crystals can be influenced by the elements associated with your zodiac sign. Earth signs may find grounding and stability through their chosen crystals, while Air signs can benefit from the clarity and communication enhancements that certain stones provide. By recognizing these elemental relationships, you can tailor your crystal usage to align with the natural flow of energy in your life. Experimenting with different crystals during various phases of your astrological journey can deepen your understanding of yourself and the universe, allowing you to use the full potential of both astrology and witchcraft in your spiritual practice.

Healing Properties of Crystals for Each Zodiac Sign

The healing properties of zodiac crystals are a captivating intersection of astrology and crystal therapy, offering practitioners a profound tool for enhancing their spiritual journeys. Each zodiac sign is associated with specific crystals that resonate with its elemental energies and personality traits. By understanding these connections, individuals can use the unique vibrational frequencies of these stones to promote healing, balance, and empowerment in their lives. This subchapter explores how these crystals not only align with astrological energies but also serve as powerful allies in various rituals and spellcasting practices.

For instance, Aries, ruled by Mars and characterized by its fiery nature, benefits greatly from the energizing properties of Carnelian. This vibrant crystal is known to stimulate motivation and courage, making it an excellent choice for those born under this sign who seek to amplify their drive. Similarly, Taurus, an earth sign, finds grounding and stability through the nurturing energies of Rose Quartz, which fosters self-love and emotional healing. By including these zodiac-specific crystals into daily practices or rituals, individuals can tap into the natural energies associated with their signs, enhancing their overall well-being.

The relationship between zodiac signs and their corresponding crystals extends beyond mere associations; it is rooted in the elemental correspondences that define each sign. For example, the air signs—Gemini, Libra, and Aquarius—can use the clarity and communication-enhancing properties of Aquamarine. This crystal aids in self-expression and helps to dispel mental fog, aligning harmoniously with the intellectual nature of air signs. Practitioners can employ these stones in meditation or during astrological rituals, elevating their spiritual practices to new heights by creating a synergy between their astrological identity and the crystals that resonate with it.

Moreover, the healing properties of zodiac crystals can be integrated into astrological rituals for manifestation. By selecting a crystal that aligns with the energies of a specific astrological event—such as a full moon or a solar eclipse—individuals can amplify their intentions and goals. For instance, during a full moon in Cancer, individuals may choose to work with Moonstone, which enhances intuition and emotional healing. This not only deepens the connection to the astrological energies at play but also reinforces the healing properties of the crystal, creating a potent environment for personal growth and transformation.

In conclusion, the healing properties of zodiac crystals offer a rich and diverse toolkit for adults interested in astrology, witchcraft, and spiritual practices. By integrating these crystals into daily rituals and spellcasting, practitioners can use the unique energies associated with their zodiac signs, facilitating healing and empowerment on multiple levels. Whether through meditation, spellwork, or simple daily use, the synergy between astrology and crystal energies presents an opportunity for deeper self-discovery and spiritual enhancement, making it an invaluable aspect of modern astrological practice.

Crafting Your Own Astrological Grimoire

Documenting personal experiences and insights is a vital practice for anyone delving into the intricate realms of astrology and witchcraft. This subchapter encourages practitioners to maintain a personal journal or grimoire, capturing their encounters with astrological influences, rituals, and spells. By chronicling these experiences, individuals can develop a deeper understanding of their own energies and how they interact with the cosmos. Documenting personal insights not only serves as a valuable reference for future practices but also fosters a sense of self-awareness and growth in one's spiritual journey.

Astrological spellcasting, which combines zodiac traits with specific spells, is particularly enriched through personal documentation. Each sign embodies distinct characteristics that can significantly influence the effectiveness of a spell. By noting the outcomes of various spells conducted under different astrological conditions, practitioners can identify patterns and refine their approaches. For example, a Leo may find success in spells related to confidence and creativity during a waxing moon, while a Pisces might resonate more during a full moon when emotions are heightened. Such observations empower individuals to customize their practices according to their unique astrological makeup, leading to more profound and personalized results.

Incorporating astrological rituals for manifestation into one's documentation further enhances this practice. Rituals aligned with significant astrological events, such as eclipses or planetary transits, can be powerful tools for manifestation. By recording the intentions set during these rituals and the subsequent outcomes, practitioners can evaluate the effectiveness of their methods over time. This reflective process allows for adjustments and improvements, tailoring future rituals to align more closely with personal goals and astrological energies. The act of writing down these experiences not only solidifies the intention but also sets the stage for accountability in one's spiritual practice.

Elemental astrology also plays a crucial role in documenting personal experiences. Each zodiac sign is associated with one of the four elements: earth, air, fire, or water, which can significantly influence a practitioner's approach to witchcraft. By noting how elemental energies affect their rituals and spells, individuals can cultivate a deeper connection with both their astrological sign and the natural world. For instance, a Capricorn, an earth sign, may find that grounding rituals yield more satisfying results, while a Sagittarius, a fire sign, may thrive in dynamic and expansive practices. Documenting these experiences can lead to a richer understanding of how elemental forces interact with personal energies.

Finally, the exploration of zodiac-based crystals and gemstones enriches the documentation process, as they can enhance both astrological practices and individual energies. Each zodiac sign resonates with specific crystals that amplify its traits and healing properties. By recording experiences with these stones—such as their effects during rituals, meditations, or daily life—practitioners can uncover which crystals work best for their unique needs. This knowledge not only deepens their understanding of their astrological identity but also empowers them to create a more effective and personalized toolkit for their spiritual journey. In essence, documenting personal experiences and insights fosters a continuous cycle of learning, growth, and empowerment in the realms of astrology and witchcraft.

Customizing Spells and Rituals

Customizing spells and rituals is an essential

aspect of integrating astrology with witchcraft, allowing practitioners to use the unique energies of their zodiac signs. Each sign possesses distinct traits, elemental associations, and planetary influences that can be leveraged to enhance spellcasting and ritual work. By tailoring spells to align with these astrological nuances, practitioners can increase their effectiveness and personal resonance. This subchapter will explore the importance of customization in spellwork, providing insights on how to create rituals that reflect the characteristics of each zodiac sign.

The first step in customizing spells is to understand the core attributes of the zodiac sign in question. Each sign embodies specific qualities, such as Aries' assertiveness, Taurus' stability, or Gemini's adaptability. By recognizing these traits, practitioners can design spells that either amplify these strengths or address weaknesses. For instance, a spell aimed at enhancing courage might be particularly effective for Aries, while a ritual for grounding and security would resonate well with Taurus. This alignment ensures that the energy invested into the spell is in harmony with the natural tendencies of the sign, leading to more profound and impactful results.

In addition to the inherent qualities of each zodiac sign, astrology also encompasses elemental associations that further enrich spell customization. The four elements—earth, air, fire, and water—correspond to specific signs and can be used to augment the potency of rituals. For example, fire signs like Leo and Sagittarius may benefit from spells that incorporate flames or heat to channel their dynamic energy, while water signs such as Cancer and Pisces may find strength in rituals involving water to enhance their emotional and intuitive capabilities. Understanding these elemental connections allows practitioners to create spells that resonate deeply with the fundamental energies of their zodiac signs.

Astrological events play a crucial role in ritual customization as well. Aligning spellwork with significant astrological occurrences—such as eclipses, solstices, or planetary transits—can amplify the desired effects of the ritual. For example, a manifestation ritual performed during a new moon can use the energy of new beginnings, while a spell for release during a full moon can facilitate letting go of old patterns. By timing rituals to coincide with these celestial events, practitioners can channel the cosmic energy available at that moment, making their work more potent and aligned with the rhythms of the universe.

Finally, including zodiac-based crystals and gemstones into customized spells adds another layer of depth to the practice. Each zodiac sign is associated with specific stones that resonate with its energies, enhancing magical workings and healing practices. For example, the nurturing qualities of

Moonstone align beautifully with Cancer, while the assertive energy of Carnelian complements the boldness of Aries. By selecting crystals that correspond to their zodiac sign, practitioners can amplify the energies of their spells, creating a harmonious connection between their intentions and the natural world. This holistic approach not only enriches the spellcasting experience but also deepens the practitioner's understanding of their astrological influences.

Incorporating Astrology into Daily Life

Incorporating astrology into daily life can deepen one's connection to the cosmos, enhance personal growth, and empower magical practices. By understanding the energetic influences of celestial bodies, practitioners of astrology and witchcraft can make informed choices that align with their spiritual paths. This subchapter explores practical ways to weave astrological insights into everyday routines, rituals, and spellcasting, ultimately enriching the experiences of those who seek to use the powers of the zodiac.

The first step in integrating astrology into daily life is to establish a consistent practice of observing astrological transits and events. Keeping an astrological calendar can help you track significant dates, such as new moons, full moons, retrogrades, and eclipses. Each of these events carries unique energies that can be utilized for specific intentions. For instance, new moons are ideal for setting intentions and initiating new projects, while full moons are perfect for releasing what no longer serves you. By aligning your activities with these celestial rhythms, you can maximize the effectiveness of your rituals and spellcasting.

Elemental astrology plays a crucial role in understanding how the four elements—earth, air, fire, and water—interact with the twelve zodiac signs. Each sign is associated with one of these elements, which can guide your choice of rituals and spells. For example, earth signs such as Taurus and Capricorn may benefit from grounding rituals that incorporate herbs and crystals like black tourmaline or moss agate. Air signs, on the other hand, may find empowerment in spells that involve communication and clarity, utilizing elements like incense or feathers. By tailoring your practices to the elemental nature of your zodiac sign, you can enhance your connection to both the earth and the universe.

In addition to rituals and spellcasting, astrology can also serve as a powerful tool for divination. Utilizing astrological charts can provide insight into future possibilities and influences in your life. Techniques such as horary astrology, which answers specific questions based on the moment the question is asked, or electional astrology, which helps choose the best time to undertake a particular action, can be incorporated into your divination practices. By combining these astrological techniques with traditional forms of divination, like tarot or runes, you can gain a more comprehensive understanding of your path and the energies surrounding you.

Using zodiac-based crystals and gemstones can amplify your astrological work. Each zodiac sign has specific stones that resonate with its energies and traits. For example, a Cancer might benefit from the nurturing qualities of moonstone, while an Aries may use the bold energy of carnelian. Incorporating these stones into your daily practices—whether through wearing jewelry, carrying them as talismans, or using them in rituals—can enhance your intention and strengthen your connection to your astrological identity. By thoughtfully integrating astrology into your life, you not only honor the celestial influences at play but also empower your spiritual journey through witchcraft and personal manifestation.

Aries Magic
March 21 - April 19

Aries Spell for Courage

Ingredients:

- Red candle
- Rosemary
- A small mirror

Instructions:

1. Light the red candle.

2. Sprinkle rosemary in a circle around the candle.

3. Look into the mirror and say, "With courage, I rise; my spirit will fly."

4. Visualize your fears dissolving, then extinguish the candle.

Aries Spell for Leadership

Ingredients:

- A piece of paper
- Pen
- Cinnamon
- A yellow candle

Instructions:

1. Write a leadership goal on paper.

2. Dust the paper with cinnamon.

3. Light the yellow candle and say, "I lead with strength and grace."

4. Burn the paper in the candle flame and visualize your success.

Aries Spell for Passion

Ingredients:

- A red rose
- Honey
- A small bowl of water

Instructions:

1. Place the red rose in the bowl of water.

2. Drizzle honey over the rose.

3. Say, "Passion flows like this sweet nectar."

4. Leave the bowl overnight to infuse your space with passion.

Prosperity Spell for Aries

Ingredients:

- Green candle (for growth and abundance)
- Cinnamon stick (for attraction and prosperity)
- A small dish of salt (for purification and protection)
- A coin (to symbolize wealth)
- Basil leaves (for prosperity and good fortune)
- A piece of paper and a pen (to write your intentions)

• A small pouch or envelope (to hold your ingredients)

Instructions:

1. Prepare Your Space: Find a quiet area where you won't be disturbed. Cleanse the space by burning sage or lighting incense. Set up your materials in front of you.

2. Ground Yourself: Take a few deep breaths to center yourself. Visualize the energy of prosperity flowing into your space.

3. Write Your Intentions: On the piece of paper, write down what prosperity means to you. Be specific about what you want to attract, whether it's financial wealth, career success, or abundance in general.

4. Create the Altar: Place the green candle in the center of your workspace. Surround it with the dish of salt, the cinnamon stick, the coin, and the basil leaves.

5. Light the Candle: As you light the green candle, say the following incantation:"By the flame of this light, I call forth abundance bright. Prosperity, come to me, As I will, so mote it be."

6. Focus Your Intentions: Hold the piece of paper with your written intentions over the flame of the candle (carefully, so it doesn't catch fire). As you do this, visualize your desires manifesting. Feel the energy of prosperity surrounding you.

7. Place the Ingredients in the Pouch: After the paper has warmed, place it in the small pouch or

envelope along with the coin, basil leaves, and a small piece of the cinnamon stick.

8.   Seal Your Intentions: Hold the pouch in your hands and say: "With this charm, I seal my fate, Prosperity comes, I shall not wait. Abundance flows, like a river wide, In my life, it shall abide."

9.   Let the Candle Burn: Allow the green candle to burn out completely if possible. If not, you can extinguish it with a candle snuffer (avoid blowing it out).

10. Keep the Pouch Safe: Place the pouch in a special place where you keep your financial documents or in a location that feels sacred to you. This will serve as a reminder of your intentions.

Repeat this spell whenever you feel the need to reinforce your prosperity intentions, ideally during a waxing moon when energy is building.

Aries Protection Spell

To create a protective shield around you, using the fiery energy of Aries to ward off negativity and promote courage.

Ingredients:

•   A red candle (symbolizing passion and strength)

•   A small piece of black tourmaline or obsidian (for grounding and protection)

•   A sprig of rosemary (for purification and protection)

- A pinch of salt (to absorb negative energy)
- A small bowl of water (to represent emotions and balance)
- A piece of paper and a pen (to write your intention)
- A fireproof dish (for burning the paper)

Instructions:

1. Choose Your Space: Find a quiet place where you won't be disturbed. Create a comfortable atmosphere by dimming the lights or playing soft music if you wish.

2. Prepare Your Space: Set up your ingredients in front of you. Place the red candle in the center, with the black tourmaline/obsidian on one side and the bowl of water on the other.

3. Ground Yourself: Take a few deep breaths, in through the nose and out through the mouth. Visualize your body becoming a strong and steady foundation, connecting you to the earth.

4. Write Your Intention: On the piece of paper, write down your intention for protection. Be specific about what you want to protect yourself from, whether it's negative energy, fear, or something else.

5. Light the Candle: Carefully light the red candle, focusing on the flame as a representation of your fiery Aries energy. Visualize the flame growing larger, surrounding you with warmth and strength.

6. Add Ingredients: Sprinkle a pinch of salt around the candle, forming a protective circle. Place

the piece of black tourmaline or obsidian near the candle, visualizing it absorbing any negativity.

7. Invoke Protection: Hold the sprig of rosemary in your hands, close your eyes, and say aloud: "With the power of Aries, I stand strong. Protect me from harm, all day long. Negative energy, be gone from my sight. Shield me in love, and fill me with light."

8. Burn the Intention: Take the piece of paper with your intention and carefully burn it in the flame of the candle (use the fireproof dish to catch any ashes). As it burns, visualize your intention being released into the universe.

9. Reflect and Release: After the paper has burned completely, dip your fingers into the bowl of water, then sprinkle a few drops around the candle. This symbolizes emotional balance and the release of negativity.

10. Close the Spell: Allow the candle to burn down completely, if possible. When you're ready, thank any energies you invoked and extinguish the candle, knowing that your protection is now in place.

11. Keep the Crystals: Carry the black tourmaline or obsidian with you, or place it in a safe space in your home as a continuous source of protection.

Repeat this spell as needed, especially during times of uncertainty or when you feel your energy is being drained. Trust in your inner strength and the protective energy surrounding you.

Healing Spell for Aries

This spell is designed to promote healing and well-being, using the energetic qualities of Aries, which include passion, courage, and vitality.

Ingredients:

• Red Candle: Represents Aries energy, passion, and strength.

• Rosemary: Known for its healing properties and ability to boost memory and clarity.

• Ginger: Promotes vitality and courage, aligning with the Aries spirit.

• Citrine Crystal: Associated with joy, energy, and healing.

• Essential Oil (Peppermint or Eucalyptus): For refreshing energy and clarity.

• Small Bowl of Water: Symbolizes cleansing and renewal.

• A piece of paper and pen: For writing your intentions.

Instructions:

1. Prepare Your Space: Find a quiet area where you won't be disturbed. Cleanse the space by burning sage or lighting incense to create a sacred atmosphere.

2. Cast Your Circle (Optional): If you practice circle casting, do so to create a protective space for your spellwork.

3. Set Up Your Altar: Place the red candle in the

center. Surround it with a small bowl of water, the rosemary, and ginger. Position the citrine crystal nearby, and have your essential oil ready.

4. Light the Candle: As you light the candle, focus on the flame and visualize it representing your inner strength and healing energy. Say aloud or in your mind, "With this flame, I ignite my healing journey."

5. Prepare the Herbs: Take a moment to hold the rosemary and ginger in your hands. Visualize their energy merging with yours. You can say, "I call upon the healing energy of rosemary and the courage of ginger to flow through me."

6. Anoint with Essential Oil: Put a drop of peppermint or eucalyptus oil on your wrists and behind your ears. Breathe in the scent, allowing it to invigorate your spirit.

7. Write Your Intentions: On the piece of paper, write down your healing intentions or what you wish to manifest in terms of well-being. Be specific and positive, using present tense as if it is already happening (e.g., "I am healthy and vibrant.").

8. Place Intentions in Water: Fold the paper and gently place it in the bowl of water. As it sinks, visualize your intentions being absorbed into the water, ready to be released into the universe.

9. Meditate: Spend a few moments in meditation, focusing on your breath and the energy surrounding you. Visualize the healing light

enveloping you, filling you with warmth and strength.

10. Close the Spell: When you feel ready, thank the energies and elements you called upon. Snuff out the candle (do not blow it out, as that can scatter your intentions).

11. Dispose of the Water: After the spell, you can pour the water outside, allowing your intentions to flow into the earth.

12. Follow Up: Keep the citrine crystal with you for a boost of positive energy and remember to take care of your physical and emotional health in the days to come.

This spell can be repeated as needed, especially during times of stress or when you feel your energy waning. Trust in the process, and allow the healing to unfold naturally.

Aries Love Spell

Ingredients:

• A red candle (to symbolize passion and energy)

• A piece of rose quartz (for love and emotional healing)

• Dried rosemary (to enhance courage and strength)

• A sprig of fresh thyme (for attraction and fidelity)

• A piece of parchment paper

- A pen (preferably red or gold)
- A small bowl of water
- A pinch of salt (for purification)
- A fireproof dish or cauldron

Instructions:

1. Preparation of Space : Find a quiet and comfortable space where you won't be disturbed. Cleanse the area by lighting the pinch of salt in the fireproof dish or cauldron, allowing the smoke to purify your space and intentions.

2. Setting the Candle : Place the red candle in front of you and light it, focusing on the flame as a representation of the passion you desire.

3. Rose Quartz Activation : Hold the piece of rose quartz in your hands. Close your eyes and visualize the love you want to attract into your life. Imagine this love being strong, passionate, and fulfilling.

4. Creating Your Intention : Take the parchment paper and write down your intentions for love. Be specific about the qualities you seek in a partner and the type of relationship you desire. Use words that evoke strong emotions.

5. Herbal Infusion : Sprinkle a bit of dried rosemary and fresh thyme over the parchment. As you do this, say aloud: "With courage and strength, I call you near, Love that's true, let it appear."

6. Water Purification : Dip your fingers into the bowl of water and sprinkle a few drops onto the

parchment, symbolizing the flow of love into your life. As you do this, visualize love flowing towards you.

7. Final Assembly : Fold the parchment paper towards you three times, encapsulating your intentions. Place it under the candle while keeping the rose quartz on top.

8. Meditation : Sit quietly and meditate on your desires for a few minutes. Focus on the flame of the candle, imagining it igniting the passion and connection you seek.

9. Closing the Spell : When you feel ready, extinguish the candle (do not blow it out; pinch it or snuff it). Keep the folded parchment and rose quartz close to you or in a special place until your intentions manifest.

10. Follow-Up : Take the herbs and bury them in your garden or a potted plant as a symbolic gesture of planting the seeds of love.

Repeat this spell whenever you feel the need to reinforce your intentions or when you want to attract love into your life.

Taurus Magic
April 20 - May 20

Taurus Spell for Abundance

Ingredients:

- Green candle
- Basil
- Coin

Instructions:

1. Light the green candle.
2. Place the basil and coin beside it.
3. Say, "Abundance is drawn to me, as I am to it."
4. Allow the candle to burn down safely.

Taurus Spell for Stability

Ingredients:

- Brown cloth
- Four pebbles
- A small plant

Instructions:

1. Arrange the pebbles in a square on the cloth.
2. Place the plant in the center.
3. Say, "Grounded and stable, I find my way."
4. Keep it in a prominent place for stability.

Taurus Spell for Love

Ingredients:

- Pink candle
- Rose petals
- Vanilla oil

Instructions:

1. Light the pink candle.

2. Sprinkle rose petals around it.

3. Anoint the candle with vanilla oil.

4. Say, "Love surrounds me, pure and true," and visualize love coming to you.

Taurus Protection Spell

Ingredients:

- Green candle (for stability and grounding)
- Black salt (for protection)
- Fresh rosemary (for strength and purification)
- Crystals: rose quartz (for love) and black tourmaline (for protection)
- Small bowl of water (to represent the earth element)
- A piece of paper and a pen (to write your intentions)
- A small pouch or cloth (to hold your ingredients)

Instructions:

1. Create a Sacred Space: Find a quiet place

where you can perform the spell without interruption. Cleanse the area by burning sage or lighting incense.

2. Set Up Your Ingredients: Arrange the green candle in front of you and place the bowl of water nearby. Surround the candle with the black salt, forming a protective circle.

3. Prepare Your Intentions: Take the piece of paper and pen. Write down the specific protection you desire, focusing on what you want to shield yourself from. Be clear and concise.

4. Infuse with Herbs: Take the fresh rosemary and hold it in your hands. Close your eyes and visualize a protective barrier surrounding you. As you do this, say aloud: "With this rosemary, I call upon strength and purification to guard me."

5. Light the Candle: Once you feel centered, light the green candle. As the flame burns, imagine it radiating a warm, protective light around you.

6. Add the Crystals: Place the rose quartz and black tourmaline near the candle, forming a triangle with them and the bowl of water. This symbolizes balance, love, and protection.

7. Seal Your Intentions: Fold the paper with your written intentions and place it under the candle. Sprinkle a little black salt over it, sealing your wishes with protective energy.

8. Meditate: Spend a few moments in meditation, focusing on the flame of the candle and

visualizing the protection enveloping you. Feel the strength of Taurus energy grounding you.

9.   Close the Spell: When you feel ready, thank any energies or deities you called upon for their assistance. Allow the candle to burn for as long as it safely can. Once finished, dispose of the paper and salt in running water or bury it in the earth.

10. Carry the Pouch: Gather the rosemary, rose quartz, and black tourmaline in the small pouch or cloth. Carry it with you to maintain the protective energy.

This spell uses the grounding energy of Taurus and the protective properties of the chosen ingredients, providing you with a shield against negativity.

Luxurious Comfort Spell for Taurus
Ingredients:
- Rose Quartz - for love and self-acceptance
- Vanilla Essential Oil - for warmth and comfort
- Coconut Milk - for nurturing and soothing properties
- Lavender Flowers - for relaxation and tranquility
- Honey - for sweetness and abundance
- Green Candles - representing growth and stability
- Soft Fabrics - such as silk or cashmere, to

create a cozy atmosphere

• A Bowl of Warm Water - for cleansing and soothing energy

• A Journal and Pen - for reflection and manifestation

Instructions:

1. Prepare Your Space: Find a quiet, comfortable location where you can perform the spell without interruptions. Set the mood by dimming the lights and playing soft music if desired. Arrange soft fabrics around you to create a luxurious atmosphere.

2. Create a Sacred Circle: Light the green candles in a circle around you. As you light each candle, focus on the stability and growth you wish to manifest. Take a moment to breathe deeply and center yourself.

3. Infuse the Water: In your bowl of warm water, add a few drops of vanilla essential oil and a spoonful of honey. Stir gently with your fingers, visualizing the warmth and sweetness enveloping you. As you do this, say: "With warmth and sweetness, I call forth, Comfort and love, from the universe's source."

4. Add Lavender: Sprinkle a handful of dried lavender flowers into the bowl, allowing their soothing properties to blend with the water. As you do this, imagine the calming energy of lavender washing over you, easing any stress or tension.

5. Ritual with Rose Quartz: Hold the rose

quartz in your hand and close your eyes. Visualize a warm, pink light radiating from the stone, filling your heart with love and self-acceptance. Say: "In this moment, I embrace my worth, Abundance and love, I bring to my hearth."

6. Coconut Milk Bath: If possible, prepare a warm bath infused with coconut milk. Pour it into the tub and immerse yourself, allowing the nurturing properties of the coconut milk to envelop your body. As you soak, reflect on the comfort you seek and the stability you desire in your life.

7. Write Your Intentions: Once you feel relaxed, take out your journal and pen. Write down your intentions for comfort, love, and stability. Be specific about what you want to manifest in your life as a Taurus. This could include financial security, nurturing relationships, or self-care practices.

8. Close the Ritual: After writing, take a few moments to meditate on your intentions. Visualize them coming to fruition. When you feel ready, extinguish the candles one by one, thanking each for its energy and light.

9. Self-Care: Conclude your spell by indulging in a moment of self-care. Perhaps enjoy a sweet treat like honey drizzled on fruit or take time to pamper yourself with a favorite activity.

10. Follow-Up: Keep your journal close and revisit your intentions regularly, allowing the energy of the spell to manifest in your life.

This spell, infused with the luxurious elements that resonate with Taurus, will help you embrace comfort and nurture your inner self.

Gemini Magic
May 21 - June 20

Gemini Spell for Communication

Ingredients:

- Blue candle
- Lavender
- A piece of clear quartz

Instructions:

1. Light the blue candle.

2. Place lavender and the quartz around the candle.

3. Say, "Words flow easily, my voice is clear."

4. Meditate for a few minutes on effective communication.

Gemini Spell for Curiosity

Ingredients:

- A notebook
- A pen
- Mint leaves

Instructions:

1. Write down three things you want to learn in the notebook.

2. Place mint leaves on top of the pages.

3. Say, "Curiosity opens my mind to new paths."

4. Keep the notebook in a visible spot.

Gemini Spell for Adaptability

Ingredients:

- Yellow candle
- A feather
- A small mirror

Instructions:

1. Light the yellow candle.

2. Hold the feather while looking into the mirror.

3. Say, "I flow like the wind, adapting with ease."

4. Visualize yourself adapting to new situations.

Gemini Love Spell

Ingredients:

- Two pink candles (representing duality and communication)
- A small piece of paper
- A pen with blue ink (symbolizing intellect and clarity)
- A sprig of lavender (for calmness and love)
- A piece of clear quartz (for clarity and amplification of intentions)
- Honey (to sweeten relationships)
- A small bowl of water (for emotional depth)

Instructions:

1. Begin by finding a quiet space where you can

focus without interruptions. Set up your altar or workspace and arrange the candles in a way that represents the Gemini symbol (the twins).

2. Light the two pink candles, visualizing the glow of love and communication surrounding you. Take a moment to center yourself and clear your mind.

3. On the piece of paper, write down the qualities you seek in a partner or the aspects of your current relationship that you wish to enhance. Be specific but open to the universe's interpretation.

4. Next, take the sprig of lavender and hold it in your hands, infusing it with your intention for calmness and love. Place it on top of the written qualities.

5. Take the clear quartz and hold it while focusing on your intention. Visualize the energy of the quartz amplifying your desires, filling the space with clarity and positive energy. Place the quartz on top of the lavender.

6. Drizzle honey over the lavender and quartz, saying a few words of affirmation, such as: "May sweetness and love flow into my life, bringing joy and connection."

7. Carefully place the bowl of water in front of the candles. This represents emotional depth and the flow of feelings. Dip your fingers into the water and sprinkle a few drops over the candles, sealing your intentions with the element of water.

8. Allow the candles to burn down safely, focusing on your intention. You can meditate or visualize the love you seek during this time.

9. Once the candles have burned out, keep the lavender and quartz in a special place as a reminder of your spell and intentions.

10. Repeat this spell on the next Gemini full moon for enhanced energy and manifestation power.

Express gratitude for the love that is coming your way, and trust the process.

Gemini Prosperity Spell

Ingredients:

- Green candle (for prosperity)
- Citrine crystal (for abundance and wealth)
- Basil (for prosperity and good fortune)
- A small piece of paper
- A pen (preferably green or gold)
- A small bowl of water
- A pinch of salt (for purification)

Instructions:

1. Preparation : Find a quiet space where you won't be disturbed. Set up your workspace by placing the green candle in the center. Surround it with the citrine crystal and a small bowl of water.

2. Cleansing : Sprinkle a pinch of salt into the bowl of water. Dip your fingers into the water and sprinkle a few drops around your workspace to cleanse the area of any negative energy.

3.   Lighting the Candle : Light the green candle and focus on its flame. Visualize it as a beacon attracting prosperity into your life.

4.   Writing Your Intent : Take the small piece of paper and write down your specific prosperity intention. Be clear and concise, stating what you wish to attract, such as a new job opportunity, financial stability, or abundance in general.

5.   Infusing with Energy : Fold the paper and hold it in your hands. Close your eyes, take a deep breath, and envision the outcome you desire. Feel the energy of abundance flowing into your life.

6.   Adding Herbs : Take a pinch of basil and sprinkle it over the folded paper. As you do this, repeat a prosperity affirmation, such as: "Abundance flows to me effortlessly."

7.   Final Steps : Place the folded paper beneath the citrine crystal. Allow the candle to burn for at least 15 minutes while keeping your focus on your intention. If possible, let it burn all the way down.

8.   Closing the Ritual : Once the candle has burned, thank the universe for the abundance that is on its way to you. Dispose of the remaining wax and any leftover herbs in a natural setting, like a garden or flower bed, to release your intentions into the world.

9.   Follow-Up : Keep the citrine crystal with you or place it in a location where you can see it daily as a reminder of the prosperity you are inviting into your life.

Perform this spell during a waxing moon phase to enhance the energy of growth and abundance.

Cancer Magic
June 21 - July 22

Cancer Spell for Emotional Healing

Ingredients:

- White candle
- Chamomile
- A bowl of saltwater

Instructions:

1. Light the white candle.
2. Add chamomile to the bowl of saltwater.
3. Say, "I cleanse my heart, I heal my soul."
4. Dip your fingers in the water for a few minutes.

Cancer Spell for Moonlit Protection

Ingredients:

- Silver candle
- Sea salt
- Moonstone
- A small bowl of water
- A piece of paper and a pen

Instructions:

1. Find a quiet space where you can focus, preferably by a window where you can see the moon.

2. Light the silver candle and place it in front of you.

3. Fill the bowl with water and sprinkle a pinch of sea salt into it, mixing it gently.

4. Take the piece of paper and write down any fears or negative energies you wish to release.

5. Hold the moonstone in your hand, close your eyes, and visualize a protective light surrounding you.

6. Dip your fingers into the salted water and sprinkle a few drops over the piece of paper, saying, "As the moon reflects in the water, I cleanse my fears away."

7. Fold the paper and place it under the candle. Let the candle burn down completely, allowing the protective energy to envelop you.

Prosperity Spell for Cancer
Ingredients:
- Green candle (for prosperity and abundance)
- A small bowl of salt (for purification)
- A piece of citrine or green aventurine (for wealth attraction)
- A coin (to symbolize financial gain)
- A piece of paper and a pen (to write your intentions)
- A small bowl of water (to represent emotions and intuition)
- A sprig of basil (for good fortune)

Instructions:

1.   Preparation : Find a quiet space where you won't be disturbed. Cleanse your area by sprinkling some salt around to create a sacred space.

2.   Setting the Mood : Light the green candle and place it in front of you. As you light it, visualize the flame bringing warmth and prosperity into your life.

3.   Focus on Your Intentions : Take the piece of paper and pen. Write down your specific intentions regarding prosperity and abundance. Be clear and concise about what you seek.

4.   Infuse the Coin : Hold the coin in your hand and envision it glowing with positive energy. As you do this, speak your intentions aloud, imagining the coin attracting wealth into your life.

5.   Add the Stones : Place the citrine or green aventurine next to the candle. These stones will help amplify your intentions. Visualize their energy connecting with the candle's flame.

6.   Water Element : Take the bowl of water and dip your fingers in it. As you do, think about how your emotions can help manifest your desires. Feel the water's energy and let it flow through you.

7.   Basil Blessing : Hold the sprig of basil close and whisper a blessing for good fortune. You can say something like, "With this basil, I call forth abundance and prosperity into my life."

8.   Final Visualization : Sit quietly for a few moments, focusing on the flame of the candle and the

energies around you. Visualize your intentions manifesting in your life, surrounded by the warmth and light of the candle.

9. Closing the Spell : When you feel ready, thank the energies and elements you've called upon. Allow the candle to burn down safely (or extinguish it if needed), keeping the coin and stones with you as a talisman for prosperity.

10. Follow Up : Place the piece of paper with your intentions somewhere special, like under your pillow or in a wallet, as a reminder of your goals.

Repeat this spell as needed, especially when you feel the energy waning or your intentions need reinforcement.

Cancer Love Spell

Ingredients:
- A small white candle
- A piece of rose quartz
- Dried lavender
- A drop of honey
- A small bowl of water

Instructions:

1. Find a quiet space where you can focus without distractions. Set up your materials in front of you.

2. Light the white candle, symbolizing purity and love.

3. Hold the rose quartz in your hands, close

your eyes, and envision the love you desire. Feel the warmth of love surrounding you.

4. Sprinkle a small amount of dried lavender around the candle. As you do this, say, "With the scent of lavender, love I attract, pure and true, bring my heart back."

5. Add a drop of honey to the bowl of water, stirring it gently. As you stir, say, "Sweetness flows, love will grow, in my heart, let it show."

6. Dip your fingers into the honeyed water and sprinkle a few drops onto the candle, while visualizing your intentions.

7. Allow the candle to burn for a while as you meditate on your intention for love. When you're ready, snuff out the candle (do not blow it out) and keep the rose quartz close to you as a reminder of your intention.

8. Dispose of the lavender and water in a natural setting, like a garden or park, to release your spell into the universe.

Repeat this spell as needed, keeping your heart open to love.

Happy Home Spell for Cancer
Ingredients:
- White candle (for purity and protection)
- Sea salt (for cleansing)
- Fresh basil (for prosperity and happiness)
- A small bowl of water (to represent

emotions)

- A piece of rose quartz (for love and harmony)

Instructions:

1. Begin by finding a quiet space in your home where you won't be disturbed. Set the mood by dimming the lights or lighting additional candles if you wish.

2. Cleanse the area by sprinkling a little sea salt around your space, creating a boundary of protection and purification.

3. Place the bowl of water in front of you, symbolizing the emotional energy within your home.

4. Light the white candle and hold it in your hands for a moment, focusing on the warmth and light it brings. Visualize it filling your home with positivity and joy.

5. Take the fresh basil and hold it close to your heart. As you do so, envision it attracting happiness and prosperity into your living space. Place the basil next to the bowl of water.

6. Finally, take the piece of rose quartz and hold it in your hands. Close your eyes and meditate on the love and harmony you want to invite into your home. After a few moments, place the rose quartz in the water, allowing it to infuse the space with its calming energy.

7. Sit quietly for a few minutes, focusing on the intention of creating a happy and harmonious home. When you feel ready, snuff out the candle (do not

blow it out) to preserve the energy.

8.   Leave the bowl of water, basil, and rose quartz in a prominent place in your home for at least 24 hours to continue attracting positive energy.

Repeat this spell whenever you feel your home needs a boost of joy and love.

Leo Magic

July 23 - August 22

Leo Spell for Radiance and Confidence

Ingredients:

- Gold candle
- Sunflower seeds
- A piece of orange fabric
- A small mirror
- Cinnamon powder

Instructions:

1. Create a comfortable space where you can sit and focus on your intentions.

2. Light the gold candle and place it in front of you.

3. Scatter a few sunflower seeds around the candle for added energy.

4. Take the piece of orange fabric and place it on your lap.

5. Hold the small mirror reflecting the light of the candle and look into it.

6. Sprinkle a pinch of cinnamon powder around the candle, invoking warmth and confidence.

7. Say aloud, "With the light of the sun, I shine

bright, radiating confidence and joy, day and night."

8. Sit quietly for a few moments, focusing on your vibrant energy before extinguishing the candle.

Leo Love Spell

Ingredients:

- A red candle
- A small piece of paper
- A pen or pencil
- A pinch of cinnamon
- A small piece of rose quartz
- A few drops of honey

Instructions:

1. Find a quiet space where you won't be disturbed. Set up your workspace by placing the red candle in front of you. Light the candle, focusing on its warm flame.

2. Take the small piece of paper and write down the qualities you desire in a partner or the feelings you wish to attract into your relationship. Be specific and positive.

3. Sprinkle a pinch of cinnamon over the paper while envisioning the passion and warmth of love surrounding you.

4. Fold the paper towards you three times, symbolizing the attraction of love into your life.

5. Place the folded paper under the rose quartz, which is known for its properties of love and harmony.

6. Add a few drops of honey onto the paper, representing sweetness in your love life.

7. Close your eyes and visualize the love you wish to attract. Imagine it flowing towards you like the warm light of the candle.

8. Let the candle burn for as long as you feel comfortable, allowing your intentions to be set into the universe.

9. Once the candle has burned out, keep the folded paper and rose quartz in a safe place as a reminder of your intentions.

Repeat this spell during a waxing moon for best results, as this is a time of growth and attraction.

Leo Protection Spell

Ingredients:

- A yellow candle (to represent Leo's fire element)
- A piece of citrine or tiger's eye (for protection and confidence)
- A few drops of essential oil (such as bergamot or frankincense)
- A small bowl of water (to symbolize emotional clarity)
- A pinch of salt (for purification)

Instructions:

1. Begin by finding a quiet space where you won't be disturbed. Arrange your ingredients in

front of you.

2.   Light the yellow candle, focusing on its flame and envisioning it as a protective barrier surrounding you.

3.   Hold the citrine or tiger's eye in your hands, and visualize its energy amplifying your strength and safeguarding you from negativity.

4.   Add a few drops of essential oil to the water in the bowl, stirring gently while speaking your intention: "With this water, I cleanse my spirit, inviting only positivity and protection."

5.   Sprinkle a pinch of salt into the water, saying: "This salt purifies and wards away harm, keeping my energy safe and calm."

6.   Place the bowl of water near the candle and the stone. Close your eyes and take a few deep breaths, allowing the energies of the ingredients to align with your intention for protection.

7.   Let the candle burn for as long as you feel comfortable, and when you're ready, extinguish it, knowing that the protection you've invoked remains with you.

Repeat this spell as needed, especially during times of stress or uncertainty, to reinforce your protective energy.

Prosperity Spell for Leo
Ingredients:
- A small piece of golden citrine (for

abundance and success)

- A green candle (for growth and prosperity)
- A pinch of cinnamon (for attraction and warmth)
- A small bowl of salt (for purification)
- A coin (to represent wealth)
- A piece of paper and a pen (to set your intentions)
- Fresh basil leaves (for prosperity and good fortune)
- A small dish of honey (for sweetness in your endeavors)
- A few drops of essential oil (such as bergamot or patchouli for attraction)
- A lion figurine or image (to represent Leo's strength and leadership)

Instructions:

1. Prepare Your Space: Find a quiet place where you won't be disturbed. Cleanse the space with the bowl of salt by sprinkling it around your working area, creating a sacred circle for your spell.

2. Set the Mood: Light the green candle and place it in front of you, symbolizing the growth of your prosperity. As you light the candle, visualize the flame bringing warmth and abundance into your life.

3. Create Your Intention: Take the piece of paper and pen. Write down a clear intention or affirmation about the prosperity you wish to attract. Be as specific as possible, focusing on what you want

to achieve. For example: "I attract abundance and success in my career and financial endeavors."

4.	Charge Your Ingredients: Hold the golden citrine in your hands and close your eyes. Visualize golden light surrounding you, filling you with confidence and attracting wealth. Pass the coin over the flame of the candle three times to charge it with your intention.

5.	Combine the Elements: In a small bowl, mix the cinnamon and fresh basil leaves. As you do this, say aloud, "With this blend, I attract prosperity and success." Place the mixture near the candle.

6.	Add Sweetness: Drizzle a small amount of honey onto your intention paper, symbolizing sweetness in your pursuits. This represents the ease with which you attract prosperity.

7.	Anoint the Candle: Add a few drops of your chosen essential oil to the candle while visualizing the oil infusing your spell with attraction and abundance. Imagine the scent enveloping you and drawing in opportunities.

8.	Invoke Leo Energy: Place the lion figurine or image next to the candle. As a Leo, you embody strength and leadership. Affirm your personal power by saying, "I am a leader of my own destiny, and I attract prosperity with my strength and confidence."

9.	Visualize Your Prosperity: Spend a few moments in meditation, focusing on your intention and visualizing your life filled with abundance. See yourself achieving your goals, feeling the joy and satisfaction that comes with it.

10. Close the Spell: After meditating, express gratitude for the prosperity that is on its way to you. Allow the candle to burn down completely, or extinguish it safely if you need to leave the space. Keep the coin and intention paper in a safe place as a reminder of your commitment to attracting prosperity.

11. Follow Up: Repeat this spell every month, ideally on the New Moon or during a waxing moon, to continuously attract and strengthen your financial and personal growth.

This elaborate spell connects Leo's natural fire and leadership qualities with the energies of abundance and prosperity. Embrace your inner strength and let it guide you toward the wealth you seek.

Popularity Spell for Leo

Ingredients:

- A small piece of gold or a gold-colored candle
- A pinch of cinnamon
- A few drops of rose oil
- A piece of yellow fabric
- A handful of sunflower seeds
- A small mirror
- A piece of paper
- A pen

Instructions:

1.   Preparation : Choose a quiet space where you can perform your spell without interruptions. Lay out your yellow fabric on a flat surface to create your sacred space.

2.   Candle Setup : Place the gold or gold-colored candle at the center of the fabric. This represents the Leo energy, radiating warmth and confidence.

3.   Cinnamon Sprinkle : Light the candle and sprinkle a pinch of cinnamon around its base. Cinnamon is known for attracting positive energy and popularity.

4.   Rose Oil : Take the rose oil and anoint the candle with a few drops, moving from the base to the top. As you do this, focus on your desire for popularity and the warmth of your Leo nature.

5.   Mirror Placement : Place the small mirror next to the candle, facing it. This symbolizes self-reflection and amplifies your personal energy, allowing you to shine brighter.

6.   Sunflower Seeds : Next, take the handful of sunflower seeds and scatter them around the candle. Sunflowers are symbols of positivity and are known to attract good fortune.

7.   Writing Your Intention : On the piece of paper, write down your intention clearly. For example, "I attract friends and positive attention effortlessly."

8.   Fold and Charge : Fold the paper and place it

beneath the mirror. This helps to reflect your intention back to the universe.

9.   Meditation : Sit comfortably and meditate for a few moments while focusing on the flame of the candle. Visualize yourself surrounded by friends and admired by others. Feel the energy of popularity flowing towards you.

10. Closing the Spell : After meditating, thank the energies and elements you called upon. Allow the candle to burn down completely if safe; otherwise, extinguish it and relight it for several days as you continue to manifest your intention.

11. Final Touch : Keep the sunflower seeds and the folded paper in a safe place, such as a special box or under your pillow, to continue drawing in popularity.

Perform this spell during a waxing moon for best results, as this phase supports growth and attraction. Remember to maintain a positive attitude and embody the confidence of the Leo spirit in your daily life.

Virgo Magic

August 23 - September 22

Virgo Spell for Clarity and Organization

Ingredients:

- Green candle
- A small notebook and pen
- Dried lavender
- A piece of clear quartz
- A bowl of earth or soil

Instructions:

1. Find a serene space where you can concentrate on your thoughts.

2. Light the green candle and place it on a flat surface in front of you.

3. Open the small notebook and write down your goals or tasks that need organization.

4. Sprinkle dried lavender around the base of the candle for clarity and calmness.

5. Hold the clear quartz in your hand, focusing on its energy as you think about your intentions.

6. Take a pinch of soil and place it in a small mound next to the candle, symbolizing growth and grounding.

7. Say, "With clarity and focus, I align my thoughts and plans to manifest my desires."

8. Allow the candle to burn while you meditate on your goals, then extinguish it when you feel ready.

Virgo Love Spell

Ingredients:

• A small piece of green aventurine (for luck and love)

• A white candle (symbolizing purity and clarity)

• Dried lavender (for calmness and attraction)

• A pinch of cinnamon (to add warmth and passion)

• A small bowl of honey (to sweeten relationships)

• A piece of paper

• A pen

Instructions:

1. Preparation: Choose a quiet space where you won't be disturbed. Cleanse your area by lighting the white candle and taking a few deep breaths to center yourself.

2. Write Your Intent: On the piece of paper, write down your intentions for love. Be specific about the qualities you seek in a partner or the type of relationship you desire.

3. Create the Mixture: In the small bowl, combine the dried lavender and a pinch of cinnamon.

As you mix them, visualize the love you want coming into your life.

4. Add Sweetness: Drizzle a small amount of honey into the mixture, saying aloud, "May this sweetness draw love to me."

5. Charge the Crystal: Hold the green aventurine in your hand and focus on your intentions. Visualize the love you desire flowing towards you. Envision the crystal absorbing all your wishes.

6. Final Assembly: Place the mixture of lavender, cinnamon, and honey in front of the candle. Set the green aventurine on top of the mixture. Light the candle and say, "With this light, I call forth love, pure and bright. Bring to me the heart that feels right."

7. Meditation: Sit quietly for a few moments, focusing on the flame and your intentions. Feel the energy of love surrounding you.

8. Closing: Once you feel complete, extinguish the candle (do not blow it out; snuff it instead). Keep the mixture and the crystal in a safe place as a reminder of your intentions.

Repeat this spell for three nights in a row, allowing the energy to build each time. Trust that the universe will bring the right love into your life.

Virgo Protection spell
Ingredients:

- A small white candle
- A piece of amethyst crystal
- Dried lavender
- A small bowl of salt
- A piece of paper
- A pen

Instructions:

1. Preparation : Find a quiet space where you will not be disturbed. Cleanse your area by lighting the white candle, symbolizing purity and protection.

2. Circle of Salt : Pour the salt into a circle on your workspace. This will act as a barrier to protect your energy while you perform the spell.

3. Amethyst Placement : Place the amethyst crystal in the center of the salt circle. Amethyst is known for its protective properties and will enhance the energy of the spell.

4. Lavender Addition : Sprinkle the dried lavender around the amethyst. Lavender helps to promote calmness and protection.

5. Writing Intentions : On the piece of paper, write down any specific concerns or energies you wish to protect yourself from. Be clear and concise about your intentions.

6. Final Assembly : Fold the paper three times and place it under the amethyst crystal, ensuring it is within the salt circle.

7. Meditation : Close your eyes and take a few deep breaths. Visualize a protective shield

surrounding you, made of white light, and feel the energy of the amethyst and lavender working together.

8.   Closing the Spell : After a few minutes of meditation, thank the energies and elements for their support. Allow the candle to burn down completely as a sign of your intentions being set.

9.   Aftercare : Keep the amethyst and the folded paper in a safe place, allowing them to continue providing protection.

This spell uses the meticulous and detail-oriented nature of Virgo, providing clarity and safety in a grounded way.

Well-Being Magical Bath Spell for Virgo
Ingredients:

- 1 cup Epsom salt
- 1 cup sea salt
- 5 drops lavender essential oil
- 5 drops chamomile essential oil
- 1 tablespoon dried rosemary
- 1 tablespoon dried mint
- Fresh lemon slices
- A small bowl of clear quartz crystals (optional)

Instructions:

1.   Preparation of the Space: Choose a quiet, peaceful space for your bath. Light some candles and play soft music if you wish to enhance the

atmosphere.

2.   Create the Bath Salts: In a mixing bowl, combine the Epsom salt and sea salt. Add the lavender and chamomile essential oils, stirring well to ensure even distribution. Incorporate the dried rosemary and mint, mixing thoroughly.

3.   Infusing the Water: Fill your bathtub with warm water, allowing it to reach a comfortable temperature. As the tub fills, sprinkle the prepared salt mixture into the water, visualizing the salts dissolving and infusing the water with calming energy.

4.   Add Fresh Ingredients: Once the tub is full, add the fresh lemon slices to the water. The citrus will uplift your spirit while the herbs promote relaxation and well-being.

5.   Optional Crystals: If using, place the clear quartz crystals around the edge of the tub or in the water. These crystals can enhance the energy of the bath, promoting clarity and healing.

6.   Immerse and Reflect: Step into the bath and allow yourself to relax. Close your eyes, take deep breaths, and meditate on your intentions for well-being. Visualize the water enveloping you in a protective, healing light.

7.   Duration: Stay in the bath for at least 20-30 minutes, allowing the ingredients to work their magic and your body to unwind.

8.   Aftercare: When you're ready, drain the water

and, if possible, dispose of the remaining herbs in nature as a gesture of gratitude. Rinse your body with fresh water to cleanse away any residual energies.

This magical bath spell is designed to help Virgos find balance, tranquility, and rejuvenation, promoting overall well-being.

Libra Magic

September 23 - October 22

Libra Spell for Balance and Harmony

Ingredients:

- Pink candle
- A small scale (or balancing object)
- A piece of rose quartz
- Fresh flowers (preferably in pairs)
- A bowl of honey

Instructions:

1. Set up a tranquil area where you can connect with the energy of balance.

2. Light the pink candle and place it in the center of your space.

3. Set the small scale or balancing object on one side of the candle.

4. Arrange the fresh flowers around the candle, placing them in pairs to symbolize harmony.

5. Hold the piece of rose quartz close to your heart, envisioning loving and harmonious energy.

6. Dip your fingers into the bowl of honey and anoint the flowers lightly, symbolizing sweetness in your relationships.

7. Say, "In balance and harmony, I find my peace, love flows freely, and my heart is at ease."

8.   Spend a few moments in meditation, focusing on the balance you wish to bring into your life, then extinguish the candle when complete.

Emotional Healing Bath Spell for Libra
Ingredients:
- 1 cup Epsom salt
- 1 cup sea salt
- 5 drops rose essential oil
- 5 drops lavender essential oil
- 1 tablespoon honey
- Fresh rose petals (preferably pink or white)
- A small bowl of water
- A candle (preferably in a calming color like pale blue or green)

Instructions:

1.   Prepare Your Space: Start by creating a calm atmosphere. Light the candle and place it near the bathtub. Dim the lights if possible to enhance relaxation.

2.   Mix the Salts: In a small bowl, combine the Epsom salt and sea salt. As you mix, envision the salts absorbing any negative energy or emotional pain you wish to release.

3.   Add Essential Oils: Add the rose and lavender essential oils to the salt mixture. Stir gently, allowing the soothing scents to fill the air. As you do this, focus on inviting peace and healing into your heart.

4.   Incorporate Honey: Add the tablespoon of

honey to the mixture, symbolizing sweetness and comfort. Honey is also believed to help ease emotional burdens. Stir well until combined.

5. Prepare the Bath: Fill your bathtub with warm water, ensuring it's a comfortable temperature. As the tub fills, sprinkle the salt mixture into the water, allowing it to dissolve completely.

6. Add Rose Petals: Gently scatter fresh rose petals onto the surface of the water. Visualize the petals as a protective barrier that surrounds you, promoting love and emotional healing.

7. Take the Bath: Once the bath is ready, step in slowly and allow the warm water to envelop you. Close your eyes and take deep, calming breaths. Focus on your heart, imagining a soft light growing with each inhale, healing any emotional wounds.

8. Set Your Intention: With the small bowl of water, dip your fingers and sprinkle a few drops onto your heart space, saying a quiet affirmation such as, "I release what no longer serves me and open my heart to healing and love."

9. Soak and Reflect: Stay in the bath for at least 20 minutes, reflecting on your feelings and allowing the healing energies of the ingredients to work through you. When ready, slowly rise and take a moment to feel gratitude for the healing process.

10. After the Bath: Drain the water, visualizing all negativity leaving you. Allow the candle to burn until it extinguishes naturally, symbolizing the

completion of your emotional healing journey.

This spell is designed to bring balance and peace, aligning with Libra's inherent need for harmony and emotional well-being.

Prosperous Partnership Spell for Libra
Ingredients:
- Green candle (for prosperity)
- Pink candle (for harmony and partnership)
- A piece of cord or string (preferably green or pink)
- A small bowl of salt (for purification)
- A few coins (to represent wealth)
- A piece of paper and a pen
- A small stone or crystal (such as green aventurine for prosperity or rose quartz for love)

Instructions:

1. Preparation : Find a quiet space where you can perform the spell without interruptions. Cleanse your space by sprinkling a bit of salt in the area to purify it.

2. Setting the Intention : Take the piece of paper and write down your intentions for the partnership. Be specific about what you seek—whether it's a business partnership, a collaboration, or a personal relationship.

3. Candle Placement : Place the green candle on one side and the pink candle on the other side of your intention paper. This symbolizes the balance between

prosperity and harmony in your partnership.

4.   Lighting the Candles : Light the green candle first, focusing on the energy of prosperity flowing into your partnership. Then, light the pink candle, envisioning love, harmony, and cooperation blossoming between you and your partner.

5.   Cord Binding : Take the piece of cord and tie three knots in it. As you tie each knot, say aloud your intentions for the partnership. For example: First knot: "May our partnership bring us prosperity." Second knot: "May we work together in harmony." Third knot: "May our bond grow stronger with trust."

6.   Offering : Place the coins in front of the candles as an offering to invite wealth into your partnership.

7.   Meditation : Spend a few moments meditating on the energy of the candles and your intentions. Visualize the successful partnership you desire.

8.   Closing the Spell : After you feel ready, extinguish the candles. You can keep the cord with you as a talisman for your partnership or place it somewhere meaningful.

9.   Gratitude : Thank any energies or deities you've invoked during the spell for their assistance.

Repeat this spell as often as needed, especially during a waxing moon when energies for growth and prosperity are heightened.

Libra Abundance Spell

Here's a simple money spell designed for those who resonate with the energies of Libra, focusing on balance and harmony in attracting financial abundance.

Ingredients:

- Green candle (representing prosperity)
- A small bowl of salt (for purification)
- A piece of paper and a pen
- A coin (any denomination)
- Cinnamon (ground or a stick)
- A small pouch or bag (preferably green or gold)
- A few fresh or dried bay leaves (for success)

Instructions:

1. Prepare Your Space: Find a quiet, undisturbed area where you can perform the spell. Cleanse the space by burning some incense or using sage.

2. Create a Circle: Place the bowl of salt in the center of your space. This will act as a barrier to protect your energy during the spell.

3. Light the Candle: Carefully light the green candle and focus on the flame. Visualize the energy of abundance and prosperity flowing towards you.

4. Write Your Intention: On the piece of paper, write down your financial goal or desire. Be specific about the amount or the type of financial abundance

you seek.

5.   Add the Ingredients: Fold the paper towards you (to draw in the energy) and place it in the small pouch. Add the coin, a pinch of cinnamon, and a few bay leaves to the pouch. Each ingredient represents a different aspect of your intention: the coin for wealth, cinnamon for attraction, and bay leaves for success.

6.   Focus Your Energy: Hold the pouch in your hands and close your eyes. Visualize your financial goals as if they have already been achieved. Feel the emotions associated with that success.

7.   Seal the Spell: As you visualize, say aloud: "With balance and harmony, I draw to me, the wealth I seek, so mote it be." Repeat this three times.

8.   Extinguish the Candle: Allow the candle to burn down safely, or if you need to extinguish it, do so without blowing it out (pinch or snuff it).

9.   Keep the Pouch: Carry the pouch with you, place it on your altar, or keep it in a special place where you can see it regularly as a reminder of your intention.

10. Express Gratitude: After completing the spell, take a moment to thank the universe for the abundance that is on its way to you.

Perform this spell during a waxing moon for the best results, which symbolizes growth and attraction.

Libra Lucky in Love Spell

Ingredients:

- A pink candle (symbolizing love and harmony)
- A small bowl of honey (representing sweetness in relationships)
- A piece of rose quartz (for attracting love)
- A sprig of fresh basil (for prosperity and attraction)
- A few drops of vanilla extract (for warmth and comfort)

Instructions:

1. Preparation:

Find a quiet space where you won't be disturbed. Set up your materials on a clean surface. Light the pink candle to create a warm, loving atmosphere.

2. Creating the Mixture: In the bowl, combine the honey and a few drops of vanilla extract. Stir gently, focusing on your intention to attract love and positive relationships into your life.

3. Charging the Rose Quartz: Hold the piece of rose quartz in your hands. Close your eyes and visualize the love you desire. Imagine it flowing to you effortlessly. After a minute, place the rose quartz in the bowl with the honey and vanilla mixture.

4. Adding the Basil: Take the sprig of fresh basil and sprinkle it over the mixture while saying, "With this herb, I attract love pure, my heart's desire, I'm sure."

5. Final Invocation: As you let the candle burn, say

aloud: "By the light of this flame, I call love to my name. Sweetness and warmth, come to me, as I will, so mote it be."

6. Closing: Allow the candle to burn down completely if safe to do so. When you're done, keep the rose quartz with you and use the honey mixture in a small ritual or simply as a reminder of your intention.

This spell is intended to align with Libra's natural charm and desire for harmony in relationships.

Libra Protection from Psychic Assault Spell
Ingredients:

- A small piece of rose quartz (for love and protection)
- A black candle (for warding off negativity)
- A small bowl of salt (for purification)
- A sprig of rosemary (for protection and clarity)
- A piece of white paper and a pen (to write your intention)
- A crystal pendant or charm (preferably black tourmaline for its protective qualities)
- A small piece of cloth (preferably in Libra's colors: pink or blue)

Instructions:

1. Prepare Your Space: Find a quiet place where you won't be disturbed. Set up an altar or a flat surface where you can lay out your ingredients. Clear

the area of any distractions.

2.   Cleanse Your Space: Sprinkle the salt in a circle around your working area to create a protective boundary. As you do this, visualize the salt absorbing any negative energy.

3.   Light the Black Candle: Focus on the flame as you light the candle. This flame represents your intention to ward off any psychic attacks. Take a few deep breaths to center yourself.

4.   Write Your Intention: On the piece of white paper, write a clear intention for protection against psychic assault. For example, "I am shielded from all negative psychic influences."

5.   Charge the Rose Quartz: Hold the rose quartz in your hands and visualize it glowing with a protective light. As you do this, repeat a mantra like, "Love and protection surround me."

6.   Incorporate Rosemary: Take the sprig of rosemary and hold it above the candle flame, letting the smoke waft around you as you say, "With this sacred herb, I invite clarity and protection."

7.   Create a Charm: Place the rose quartz, the crystal pendant or charm, and the written intention on the piece of cloth. Gather the corners of the cloth together, creating a small pouch. Tie it securely with a string or ribbon.

8.   Close the Ritual: Thank the energies or spirits you invoked during the spell. Let the candle burn down safely, or extinguish it if necessary (do not

blow it out, as this can scatter your intention; instead, snuff it out).

9.   Keep the Charm Close: Carry the pouch with you, or place it in a safe space in your home to maintain the protective energy.

10.   Revisit as Needed: Repeat this spell whenever you feel the need for extra protection or after experiencing any negative psychic encounters.

By following these steps, you will create a protective barrier to shield yourself from psychic assaults, aligning with the balanced and harmonious energy of your Libra nature.

Scorpio Magic

October 23 - November 21

Scorpio Spell: Shadow Embrace

Ingredients:

- A black candle
- A piece of obsidian or jet
- A sprig of rosemary
- A small bowl of water
- A piece of paper and a pen

Instructions:

1. Find a quiet space where you can focus without distractions. Light the black candle to represent the transformative energy of Scorpio.

2. Hold the piece of obsidian or jet in your hands, closing your eyes and visualizing your inner strength and power.

3. On the piece of paper, write down a fear or negative emotion you wish to release. Be specific.

4. Dip the rosemary in the bowl of water, then sprinkle some of the water over the piece of paper while saying, "With this water, I cleanse my fear, releasing what no longer serves me here."

5. Fold the paper and place it under the candle.

Allow the candle to burn down safely, visualizing the release of your negative emotion as the wax melts.

6.   Once the candle has burned down, bury the paper and any remnants in the earth as a final act of letting go.

Transformation Spell for Scorpio
Ingredients:
- Black candle (for protection and transformation)
- A small piece of obsidian or smoky quartz (for grounding)
- A sprig of rosemary (for purification)
- A small bowl of water (symbolizing emotional depth)
- A pinch of salt (for cleansing)
- A piece of paper and a pen (to write your intention)

Instructions:
1.   Preparation: Find a quiet space where you won't be disturbed. Set up an altar or a flat surface and arrange the ingredients in a circle.

2.   Cleansing: Light the black candle and place it in front of you. Hold the piece of obsidian or smoky quartz in your hand, close your eyes, and take three deep breaths. Visualize any negative energy being absorbed by the stone.

3.   Purification: Sprinkle a pinch of salt into the bowl of water. As you do so, say: "With this salt, I

purify my intentions, aligning with the energies of transformation."

4.   Intention Setting: Take the piece of paper and write down what you wish to transform in your life. It could be a habit, emotion, or situation. Be specific and clear.

5.   Invocation: Hold the paper above the candle flame (carefully, not too close) and say: "As the flame burns bright, I release what no longer serves me, embracing the power of change."

6.   Finalizing the Spell: Place the paper in the bowl of water, allowing it to soak. As the paper disintegrates, visualize your transformation taking place. Focus on the emotions and changes you wish to manifest.

7.   Closure: Extinguish the candle once you feel the energy has been released. Keep the obsidian or smoky quartz with you as a reminder of your intention and transformation.

8.   Reflection: Over the next few days, take time to meditate on your intention and remain open to the changes that will come.

This spell uses Scorpio's innate power of transformation and depth, helping you to embrace the changes you wish to see in your life.

write a short taking controlling the situation spell for scorpio, include list of ingredients and instructions.

Scorpio Spell for Taking Control of a Situation

This spell is designed to help Scorpios use their natural intensity and determination to take control of a situation that feels overwhelming or chaotic.

Ingredients:

- Black candle (for protection and power)
- Red candle (for passion and determination)
- A small piece of obsidian (for grounding and protection)
- A few drops of essential oil (like patchouli or sandalwood, for attraction and focus)
- A piece of paper and pen
- A small bowl of salt (for purification)
- A fire-safe container (for burning the paper)
- A quiet, undisturbed space

Instructions:

1. Preparation: Find a quiet space where you won't be interrupted. Set up your area by placing the black candle on your left side and the red candle on your right side. Light them both to create a focused and powerful energy.

2. Grounding: Hold the piece of obsidian in your hand. Close your eyes and take a few deep breaths, focusing on the weight of the stone and visualizing it absorbing any negativity around you.

3. Writing Intention: On the piece of paper, write down the specific situation you want to take control of. Be clear and concise about your desires and intentions.

4.   Anointing: Add a few drops of the essential oil to your fingertips and anoint the paper by rubbing the oil along the edges, infusing it with your intention.

5.   Salt Circle: Sprinkle a small amount of salt in a circle around the candles. This creates a protective boundary for your spellwork.

6.   Invocation: Hold the paper in both hands and speak your intention out loud, stating clearly what you want to manifest. For example, "I call upon my inner strength to take control of [specific situation]. I am empowered, focused, and unstoppable."

7.   Burning the Paper: Carefully light the paper with the flame from the red candle and place it in the fire-safe container. As it burns, visualize your intention being released into the universe, transforming into the energy needed to take control.

8.   Closing: Allow the candles to burn down safely. Once you feel the energy has been released, thank any spiritual energies or deities you may have called upon. Let the obsidian remain in your space to continue absorbing negativity and grounding your energy.

9.   Follow-Up: Carry the obsidian with you for a few days as a reminder of your intention and strength. Revisit your intention periodically to reinforce your power.

This spell uses Scorpio's natural intensity, helping

to channel that energy into taking decisive action in challenging situations.

Scorpio Love Attraction Spell

Ingredients:

- A red candle (for passion)
- A small piece of rose quartz (for love)
- A few drops of vanilla essential oil (for sweetness)
- A piece of paper and a pen (to write your intentions)
- A small bowl of water (to represent emotions)
- A pinch of salt (for purification)

Instructions:

1. Preparation: Find a quiet space where you won't be disturbed. Set up your materials in front of you. Light the red candle to create a warm, inviting atmosphere.

2. Cleansing: Sprinkle a pinch of salt into the bowl of water, stirring it gently to purify the space and your intentions.

3. Writing Intentions: Take the piece of paper and write down what qualities you desire in a lover. Be specific but positive. For example, "I attract a loving and passionate partner who respects me."

4. Infusing Energy: Anoint the rose quartz with a few drops of vanilla essential oil, focusing on your intention. Hold the stone in your hands, close your

eyes, and visualize the love you want to attract. Feel the energy of love surrounding you.

5. Combining Elements: Place the piece of paper with your written intentions under the bowl of water. Then, place the rose quartz on top of the paper. As you do this, say a simple affirmation, such as, "With this spell, I attract love and passion into my life."

6. Meditation: Spend a few moments in meditation, visualizing your ideal partner and the connection you desire. Feel the emotions associated with this love.

7. Closing: Allow the candle to burn down safely. Keep the rose quartz with you as a talisman, and revisit your intentions whenever you feel the need to re-energize your attraction.

8. Release: After the spell is complete, gently dispose of the paper in flowing water or bury it in the earth to release your intentions into the universe.

Use this spell with positive intentions and an open heart, and let the universe bring the love you seek.

write an aura cleansing bath spell for scorpio, include list of ingredients and instructions.

Aura Cleansing Bath Spell for Scorpio
Ingredients:
- Sea salt (1 cup)
- Epsom salt (1 cup)

- Dried lavender (1/2 cup)
- Dried rosemary (1/2 cup)
- A few drops of essential oil (lavender or eucalyptus)
- Black candle (for protection)
- White candle (for purification)
- A small bowl of water
- A clear quartz crystal (optional, for amplifying energy)
- Fresh flowers (such as white roses or chrysanthemums, optional)

Instructions:

1. Preparation: Choose a time when you can be undisturbed, preferably during a waning moon for releasing negativity. Clean your bathing area, ensuring it feels inviting and serene.

2. Create a Sacred Space: Light the black candle on your left side and the white candle on your right side. This symbolizes balance between protection and purification. If you have fresh flowers, place them around the candles to enhance the energy.

3. Fill the Bath: Fill your bathtub with warm water, ensuring it's comfortable for you. As the tub fills, visualize the water pulling away negativity.

4. Add Ingredients: Pour the sea salt and Epsom salt into the water, stating your intention aloud as you do so, such as: "With this salt, I cleanse my aura and release all that no longer serves me." Sprinkle the dried lavender and rosemary into the bath,

symbolizing peace and protection. Add a few drops of your chosen essential oil, breathing in the calming scent.

5. Crystal Charging (optional): If using a clear quartz, hold it in your hands, close your eyes, and focus on charging it with your intention for cleansing your aura.

6. Bath Ritual: Step into the bath, feeling the warm water embrace you. Take deep breaths, inhaling the soothing aroma. As you soak, visualize any negativity or tension dissolving into the water. Imagine your aura becoming brighter and lighter with each breath. Spend at least 20-30 minutes in the bath, allowing the herbs and salts to work their magic. You can meditate or quietly repeat affirmations like: "I release what no longer serves me. I am cleansed and renewed."

7. Closing the Ritual: When ready, drain the tub, imagining the release of all negativity down the drain. As you stand up, visualize a protective bubble surrounding you, created by the energies of the candles and herbs Extinguish the candles, thanking them for their assistance in your cleansing.

8. Post-Bath Care: Rinse off with fresh water to remove any remaining bath ingredients. Keep the clear quartz crystal with you or place it in your living space to continue the aura cleansing energy.

This ritual can be done regularly to maintain a clear and vibrant aura, especially beneficial for

Scorpio's intense emotional nature.

Sagittarius Magic
November 22 - December 21

Sagittarius Quest Spell

Ingredients:

- A yellow candle
- A piece of citrine
- A pinch of dried sage
- A map or globe
- A small bowl of salt

Instructions:

1. Set up your space with the yellow candle in the center, symbolizing optimism and adventure. Light the candle.

2. Place the piece of citrine next to the candle to attract abundance and new experiences.

3. Sprinkle a pinch of dried sage around the candle, creating a circle, to purify your space and invite clarity.

4. Take the map or globe and hold it in your hands, visualizing a journey or adventure you wish to embark on.

5. As you focus on your desired adventure, say, "With the fire of this flame, I call forth my quest, to

travel and explore, I'll be truly blessed."

6.　Dip your fingers into the bowl of salt and sprinkle it around the candle, sealing your intention. Let the candle burn for at least an hour, envisioning your adventures manifesting.

write a short safe travel talisman spell for sagittarius, include list of ingredients and instructions.

Sagittarius Talisman Spell for Safe Travel
Ingredients:
- A small pouch or cloth bag (preferably in shades of purple or blue)
- A piece of citrine or yellow topaz (stones associated with Sagittarius)
- A pinch of salt (for protection)
- A small piece of paper and pen
- A sprig of rosemary (for safe travels)
- A few drops of lavender essential oil (to promote calmness)
- A candle (yellow or white)

Instructions:

1.　Preparation: Find a quiet space where you won't be disturbed. Lay out all your ingredients in front of you.

2.　Cleansing the Space: Light the yellow or white candle to create a sacred atmosphere. Take a moment to breathe deeply and center yourself.

3.　Writing Your Intent: On the piece of paper,

write a short affirmation or intention for safe travels, such as "I am protected on my journey" or "I travel with safety and ease."

4.   Assembling the Talisman: Place the piece of citrine or yellow topaz in the pouch. Add the pinch of salt, the sprig of rosemary, and the piece of paper with your intention.

5.   Anointing: Add a few drops of lavender essential oil to the inside of the pouch or on the stones, visualizing calm and safe travels as you do so.

6. Sealing the Talisman: Close the pouch securely. Hold it in your hands and say a few words of gratitude for protection and safe journeys.

7.   Charging the Talisman: Allow the candle to burn for a while while you focus on your pouch. Visualize yourself traveling safely and joyfully.

8.   Final Touch: Once you feel ready, snuff out the candle (do not blow it out). Keep the talisman with you whenever you travel, whether it's in your bag, pocket, or around your neck.

This talisman will serve as a reminder of your intention and a source of protection during your journeys. Safe travels!

Abundance Spell for Sagittarius
Ingredients:
- Green candle (for prosperity)
- Bay leaf (for manifestation)
- Cinnamon stick (for attraction)

- Small bowl of salt (for purification)
- A piece of paper and a pen
- A small pouch (to hold your ingredients)

Instructions:

1. Prepare Your Space: Find a quiet area where you can work without interruptions. Light some incense or play soft music if it helps you focus.

2. Cleansing: Take the small bowl of salt and sprinkle a little around your workspace to purify the area. You can also hold the green candle in your hands and visualize it absorbing any negative energy.

3. Writing Your Intention: On the piece of paper, write down what abundance means to you. Be specific about what you want to attract into your life (ex. financial freedom, love, health).

4. Candle Ritual: Place the green candle in front of you. Light it while focusing on your intention written on the paper. Visualize the abundance flowing into your life as the candle burns.

5. Adding Ingredients: Take the bay leaf and cinnamon stick and hold them in your hands. Close your eyes and visualize your desires coming to fruition. When you feel ready, place them next to the candle.

6. Final Touch: Fold the piece of paper with your intention and place it in the pouch along with the bay leaf and cinnamon stick. You can also add a pinch of salt for purification.

7. Closing the Spell: Allow the candle to burn

down safely. As it does, repeat a positive affirmation related to abundance, such as "I attract abundance effortlessly" or "I am open to all the blessings in my life."

8.   Keep it Safe: Once the candle has burned out, carry the pouch with you or keep it in a special place to remind you of your intentions.

Repeat this spell whenever you feel the need to refresh your intentions or when the moon is waxing to enhance your manifestation power.

Sagittarius Love Spell
Ingredients:
- A red candle (symbolizing passion)
- A piece of parchment paper
- A pink or red string or cord (about 12 inches long)
- A small bowl of water
- A pinch of cinnamon (for attraction)
- A rose quartz crystal (for love)

Instructions:

1.   Preparation: Find a quiet space where you won't be disturbed. Set up your ingredients in a circle around you, placing the red candle in the center.

2.   Candle Lighting: Light the red candle and take a moment to focus on its flame. Visualize the fiery nature of Sagittarius, full of adventure and passion.

3.   Writing Your Intent: On the piece of

parchment paper, write down the qualities you seek in a partner or the type of love you wish to attract. Be specific but keep it positive.

4. Cinnamon Sprinkle: Sprinkle a pinch of cinnamon over the parchment, envisioning it enhancing your attraction and drawing love towards you.

5. Cord Tying: Take the pink or red string and hold it in your hands. As you tie three knots in the cord, say aloud what you desire in love for each knot. For example, "With this knot, I attract passion; with this knot, I invite joy; with this knot, I welcome adventure."

6. Water Offering: Dip the tied cord into the bowl of water, symbolizing the flow of love into your life. Hold it over the water and say, "As this water flows, so does love come to me."

7. Crystal Charge: Place the rose quartz crystal next to the candle and visualize it absorbing the energy of your spell.

8. Closing: Allow the candle to burn down safely while you sit in meditation, focusing on the love you wish to attract. When you feel ready, extinguish the candle, thanking the universe for its assistance.

9. Final Steps: Keep the tied cord and rose quartz close to you, such as in a pocket or under your pillow, as a reminder of your intention.

Repeat this spell during a waxing moon for best

results, using the Sagittarian spirit of exploration and openness to new love.

Capricorn Magic
December 22 - January 19

Capricorn Spell for Grounded Ambition

Ingredients:

- A green candle
- A piece of quartz crystal
- A small handful of soil or earth
- A piece of paper and a pencil
- A string or ribbon

Instructions:

1. Create a stable and quiet environment. Light the green candle to symbolize growth and ambition.

2. Hold the quartz crystal in your hands, focusing on its clarity and energy to enhance your aspirations.

3. On the piece of paper, write down a goal or ambition you wish to achieve. Be clear and concise.

4. Take the soil or earth and place it in a small bowl. As you do this, say, "From the ground I rise, with patience and care, my dreams take root in the earth's gentle share."

5. Fold the paper with your goal and bury it in the soil, visualizing it taking root and growing.

6.   Tie the string or ribbon around the bowl, symbolizing the binding of your intention. Allow the candle to burn down, affirming your commitment to your ambitions as you nurture your goal in the coming days.

Success Talisman Spell for Capricorn

This spell is designed to use the ambitious and disciplined nature of Capricorn to attract success and prosperity.

Ingredients:

- A small piece of green aventurine or citrine (crystals known for prosperity)
- A sprig of rosemary (for wisdom and remembrance)
- A pinch of cinnamon (to attract wealth)
- A small piece of paper and a pen (to write your intentions)
- A gold or green candle (representing abundance and success)
- A small bowl of water (to represent emotions and intuition)
- Incense (preferably patchouli or sandalwood for prosperity)
- A safe, quiet space to perform the spell

Instructions:

1.   Preparation of Space: Find a quiet area where you won't be disturbed. Cleanse the space by lighting the incense and allowing the smoke to purify the

surroundings. You may also want to visualize a protective circle around yourself.

2.   Setting Intentions: Take the piece of paper and write down your specific goals or intentions regarding achievement and prosperity. Be clear and concise. Fold the paper and set it aside.

3.   Candle Preparation: Place the gold or green candle in front of you. Light it, focusing on the flame as a symbol of your ambition and drive. Visualize the flame igniting your desires for success.

4.   Creating the Talisman: In the small bowl of water, add the rosemary sprig. As you do this, say: "Wisdom and remembrance guide my way, as I strive for success each day."

5.   Combining Ingredients: Place the crystal (aventurine or citrine) on top of the folded paper. Sprinkle a pinch of cinnamon over the crystal and paper, saying: "With this spice, I attract wealth, abundance, and all forms of health."

6.   Charging the Talisman: Hold the crystal and paper in your hands. Close your eyes and visualize your goals coming to fruition. Feel the energy of success flowing through you. Focus on the determination and strength of Capricorn, allowing it to empower your intentions.

7.   Final Blessing: After a few minutes, gently place the rosemary sprig in the bowl of water, along with the crystal and paper. Say: "As the earth is strong, so shall I be; with this talisman, my goals I

will see."

8.   Closing the Spell: Allow the candle to burn down safely (never leave it unattended). Keep the talisman (paper and crystal) in a special place where you can see it daily, to remind you of your intentions.

9.   Gratitude: Take a moment to express gratitude for the energy and support of the universe, acknowledging the hard work you will put in to achieve your goals.

This talisman spell can be repeated as needed or when you feel the need to recharge your intentions. Remember to stay focused and committed to your goals as you embody the Capricorn spirit of perseverance and ambition.

Love Spell for a Stable Relationship for Capricorn
Ingredients:
- One small green candle (symbolizing stability and growth)
- A piece of rose quartz (for love and compassion)
- A sprig of rosemary (for fidelity and remembrance)
- A small bowl of salt (for purification)
- A piece of paper and a pen
- A few drops of essential oil (like lavender or bergamot for harmony)
- A small pouch or cloth to hold the ingredients

Instructions:

1. Choose the Right Time: Perform this spell during a waxing moon, which is ideal for growth and attraction. Preferably on a Friday, the day associated with love.

2. Create a Sacred Space: Find a quiet space where you won't be disturbed. Cleanse the area by burning sage or lighting incense, and set up your materials on a clean surface.

3. Light the Candle: Place the green candle in front of you and light it. As you do, focus on your intention for stability and growth in your relationship. Visualize the bond you share, growing stronger and more resilient.

4. Prepare the Paper: Take the piece of paper and write down your wishes for the relationship. Be specific about what you desire—trust, communication, support, etc.

5. Charge the Ingredients: Hold the rose quartz in your hand and envision it glowing with loving energy. Pass the rosemary through the candle flame (carefully!) and say, "With this herb, I invoke loyalty and love."

6. Combine Ingredients: Place the rose quartz, rosemary, and paper into the bowl. Add a pinch of salt for purification. As you do this, say aloud: "With these elements, I bind our love in trust and harmony."

7. Add Essential Oil: Add a few drops of the

essential oil to the mixture, imagining the scent infusing the bond with peace and understanding.

8. Seal the Pouch: Place everything into the small pouch or cloth, tying it securely. As you do this, visualize the energy of your relationship being encapsulated within.

9. Close the Spell: Allow the candle to burn down completely (if safe to do so) while focusing on your intentions. If you need to extinguish it, do so without blowing it out, using a candle snuffer or pinching it.

10. Keep the Pouch: Store the pouch in a safe place, such as under your bed or in a drawer, to continue to attract stability and love into your relationship.

Revisit your intentions regularly and nurture your relationship with care and understanding.

Capricorn Sleep Spell for Recovery from Work
Ingredients:
- One small bowl of salt (for purification)
- A white candle (for clarity and focus)
- A sprig of rosemary (for memory and restful sleep)
- A piece of amethyst (for calming energy)
- A few drops of lavender essential oil (for relaxation)
- A comfortable blanket or pillow (to enhance comfort)

• A piece of paper and a pen (to write intentions)

Instructions:

1. Prepare Your Space : Find a quiet and comfortable area where you won't be disturbed. Arrange your items in a circle, placing the white candle at the center.

2. Create a Relaxing Atmosphere : Light the white candle to symbolize clarity and focus. Take a moment to breathe deeply and center yourself. Visualize any stress or fatigue melting away.

3. Purification : Take the bowl of salt and sprinkle a small amount around the candle. As you do this, say, "With this salt, I purify my space and mind, releasing all burdens I've left behind."

4. Add the Rosemary : Take the sprig of rosemary and hold it in your hands. Close your eyes and envision it absorbing your stress. After a minute, place it near the candle, saying, "Rosemary, bring me rest, for I seek to renew and refresh."

5. Incorporate the Amethyst : Hold the piece of amethyst in your hand. Picture its calming energy surrounding you. Place it next to the rosemary and say, "Amethyst, bring tranquility, guiding my dreams and easing my mind."

6. Use the Lavender : Take the lavender essential oil and put a few drops on your wrists or the pillow. Inhale the soothing scent deeply. As you do, declare, "Lavender of night, bring me peace, as I drift into

slumber, let worries cease."

7. Set Your Intentions : On the piece of paper, write down what you wish to release from your day's work and your intention for a restful sleep. This could be something like, "I release all stress and embrace restful sleep."

8. Final Visualization : Hold the paper in your hands, close your eyes, and visualize yourself waking up refreshed and rejuvenated. Imagine the stress leaving your body as you breathe out slowly.

9. Seal the Spell : Place the paper under the candle and let it burn for a while (safely monitored). Allow the candle to burn out completely if possible, or extinguish it when you feel ready and keep the paper in a safe place.

10. Sleep : Wrap yourself in the comfortable blanket or use the pillow, letting the energies of the spell and your intentions envelop you as you drift off to sleep, knowing you will wake up refreshed and renewed.

Repeat this spell as needed to enhance your recovery from work fatigue and restore balance.

Aquarius Magic

January 20 - February 18

Aquarius Spell: "Winds of Change"
Ingredients:

- 1 blue candle
- 1 small bowl of water
- 3 sprigs of fresh mint
- A pinch of sea salt
- A piece of paper and a pen

Instructions:

1. Begin by finding a quiet space where you won't be disturbed.

2. Light the blue candle to represent the innovative and humanitarian spirit of Aquarius.

3. Fill the bowl with water and place it in front of the candle.

4. Take the piece of paper and write down three changes you wish to manifest in your life.

5. Fold the paper and place it under the bowl of water.

6. Sprinkle the sea salt into the water, symbolizing purification and clarity.

7. Add the mint sprigs to the water,

representing fresh ideas and new beginnings.

8.   Spend a few moments visualizing the changes you've written down, allowing the energy to flow from the candle into the water.

9.   Let the candle burn for at least 30 minutes while focusing on your intentions.

10. Once completed, keep the paper in a safe place and pour out the water outside, symbolizing the release of your intentions into the universe.

Aquarius Love Spell for Emotional Availability
Ingredients:

• A blue candle (representing communication and clarity)

• A piece of amethyst or aquamarine crystal (for emotional balance)

• A small bowl of water (symbolizing emotions)

• A few fresh lavender sprigs (for calm and connection)

• A piece of paper and a pen (to write your intentions)

• A pinch of salt (to purify and protect)

• Optional: A few drops of essential oil (such as bergamot or rose) for uplifting energy
Instructions:

1.   Preparation: Find a quiet space where you won't be disturbed. Make sure you have all your ingredients ready. Cleanse your space by burning sage

or incense if you wish.

2.   Create Your Altar: Set up your ingredients in front of you. Place the blue candle in the center, surrounded by the lavender sprigs and the bowl of water.

3.   Light the Candle: Focus on the flame as you light the blue candle. Visualize it illuminating your path toward emotional availability and deeper connections.

4.   Write Your Intentions: Take the piece of paper and pen. Write down what emotional availability means to you and the qualities you wish to embody. Be specific about the changes you want to see in yourself.

5.   Infuse with Energy: As you write, hold the amethyst or aquamarine crystal in your hand. Visualize its energy flowing into your intentions, helping you become more open and connected emotionally.

6.   Add to the Bowl: Fold the piece of paper and place it into the bowl of water. Add a pinch of salt to the water, symbolizing purification. As you do this, say a few affirmations or a short incantation, such as: "With this water, I cleanse my heart, Open my spirit, and make a fresh start. I embrace my feelings, let them flow, To connect with others, help me grow."

7. Lavender Ritual: Take the lavender sprigs and gently crush them in your hands, releasing their calming scent. Hold them over the bowl of water and

say: "With this lavender, I invite peace, Emotional openness, let my heart release."

8. Visualize: Spend a few moments in meditation, visualizing yourself being emotionally available and connecting with others on a deeper level. Picture the feelings you want to share, the conversations you want to have, and the connections you wish to build.

9. Conclude the Ritual: Let the candle burn down safely, or extinguish it if you need to leave it unattended. Dispose of the water and paper in a natural body of water or bury it in the earth, symbolizing your commitment to this transformation.

10. Reflect: Take time after the ritual to reflect on your feelings and any insights that arise. Journaling your experiences can help solidify your intentions and track your growth.

Repeat this spell as needed, especially during the new moon or when you feel the need for a boost in emotional connection.

Social Change Spell for Aquarius

This spell is to inspire and promote social change, aligning with the progressive and humanitarian spirit of Aquarius.

Ingredients:

- Blue candle (symbolizing communication and clarity)
- Clear quartz crystal (for amplification of

intentions)

- Dried lavender (for peace and harmony)
- A piece of paper and a pen (to write your intentions)
- A small bowl of water (representing emotions and intuition)
- A pinch of salt (for purification)
- A sprig of fresh mint (for freshness and new ideas)
- Incense (preferably sandalwood or jasmine for clarity and inspiration)

Instructions:

1. Prepare Your Space: Find a quiet place where you won't be disturbed. Cleanse the space by burning incense and allowing the smoke to envelop you, setting the intention for clarity and focus.

2. Set Up Your Altar: Arrange the blue candle, clear quartz, dried lavender, bowl of water, and mint on a flat surface. Place the piece of paper and pen nearby.

3. Light the Candle: As you light the blue candle, visualize it igniting your passion for social change. Focus on the flame and express gratitude for the ability to make a difference.

4. Write Your Intentions: On the piece of paper, write down your intentions or specific changes you wish to inspire. Be clear and concise.

5. Anoint with Water and Salt: Take the bowl of water and add a pinch of salt. Stir the mixture gently,

then dip your fingers in the water and sprinkle a few drops over the paper, symbolizing purification and emotional alignment with your goals.

6. Add the Lavender and Mint: Place the dried lavender and fresh mint next to the paper, creating a small offering. As you do this, envision the peace and freshness that social change can bring to your community.

7. Hold the Clear Quartz: Take the clear quartz crystal in your hands, close your eyes, and meditate on your intentions. Visualize the energy of the crystal amplifying your commitment and the impact you want to have.

8. Focus on Your Intentions: Spend a few moments in silence, holding the crystal, and envision the change you wish to see. Imagine it unfolding in the world around you.

9. Close the Spell: When you feel ready, thank the elements and energies you've called upon. Extinguish the candle, symbolizing that your intentions are now set into motion.

10. Take Action: After the spell, take tangible steps towards your goals. Share your ideas with others, get involved in community efforts, or start a conversation about the changes you wish to see.

Keep the paper with your intentions somewhere visible as a reminder of your commitment to social change. Revisit the spell whenever you feel the need to reignite your passion for making a difference.

Protection from Harm Spell for Aquarius

Ingredients:

- A small piece of black tourmaline or obsidian (for grounding and protection)
- A sprig of rosemary (for purification and protection)
- A piece of clear quartz (to amplify intentions)
- A white candle (symbolizing purity and safety)
- A bowl of salt (to absorb negative energies)
- A small bowl of water (to represent emotional clarity)
- A piece of paper and a pen (to write your intention)

Instructions:

1. Create Your Space: Find a quiet place where you can perform the spell without interruptions. Cleanse the space by burning incense or using sage to clear any negative energy.

2. Set Up Your Altar: Arrange the black tourmaline or obsidian, rosemary, clear quartz, white candle, bowl of salt, and bowl of water on a flat surface. Place the bowl of salt in the center, surrounded by the other items.

3. Light the Candle: Light the white candle to symbolize your intention for protection. As you do this, focus on the flame and visualize a protective barrier surrounding you.

4.   Write Your Intention: Take the piece of paper and pen. Write down your intention clearly, such as "I am protected from harm and negativity." Be specific about what you wish to protect yourself from.

5.   Charge the Ingredients: Hold the black tourmaline or obsidian in your hands and say, "With this stone, I ground myself and shield my spirit." Then, take the rosemary and say, "With this herb, I purify my surroundings and create a protective space." Finally, hold the clear quartz and say, "With this crystal, I amplify my intention for safety and well-being."

6.   Combine the Elements: Sprinkle a pinch of salt into the bowl of water, representing the cleansing of emotional turmoil and negative energies. Dip the rosemary into this mixture, allowing it to absorb the protective energy.

7.   Seal the Spell: Place the written intention under the bowl of salt and water. Visualize your intention being absorbed into the bowl, enhancing its protective qualities.

8.   Close the Ritual: Allow the candle to burn for a while as you meditate on your intention. When you feel ready, extinguish the candle (do not blow it out; use a candle snuffer or pinch it out). Thank the energies and elements you called upon and express gratitude for their protection.

9.   Keep the Items: After the ritual, keep the

black tourmaline or obsidian with you, or place it in a safe space in your home. The salt and water can be disposed of outside, symbolizing the release of negativity.

Perform this spell whenever you feel the need for extra protection, especially during times of stress or uncertainty. Trust in your ability to create a shield of safety around you.

Tea Spell for Aquarius to Commune with the Muse

Ingredients:

- 1 teaspoon of dried lavender (for tranquility and inspiration)
- 1 teaspoon of dried chamomile (for calming and openness)
- 1 teaspoon of dried peppermint (to stimulate the mind and enhance creativity)
- 1 teaspoon of dried rosemary (for clarity and connection to the divine)
- Honey (to sweeten your intentions)
- A pinch of salt (to purify and ground your energy)
- Fresh lemon slice (to invigorate and uplift)
- A clear glass or ceramic teapot or mug
- A small piece of paper and a pen (to jot down insights)

Instructions:

1. Preparation of Space: Find a quiet,

comfortable space where you can relax and focus. Dim the lights or light a candle to create an inviting atmosphere.

2. Gather Your Ingredients: Place all your ingredients in front of you. Take a moment to connect with each item, acknowledging its properties and how it will contribute to your spell.

3. Boil Water: Heat water in a kettle until it reaches a rolling boil. As the water heats, visualize your intentions for the spell, focusing on inviting your muse to connect with you.

4. Combine Ingredients: In your teapot or mug, add the dried lavender, chamomile, peppermint, and rosemary. As you add each herb, say aloud or silently the intention you have for each one, such as "Lavender, bring me peace and inspiration."

5. Pour Water: Once the water is boiling, carefully pour it over the herbs. As you do this, visualize the steam rising and carrying your intentions to the universe.

6. Infusion Time: Cover the teapot or mug with a lid or a small plate to keep the heat in. Allow the tea to steep for about 7-10 minutes, during which time you can meditate or focus on your creative thoughts.

7. Strain and Sweeten: After steeping, strain the tea into another cup, if necessary. Add honey to sweeten your brew, and a few grains of salt to purify the energy. Stir gently with a spoon, visualizing the blend of flavors and intentions harmonizing.

8. Add Lemon: Squeeze a slice of fresh lemon into your tea, stirring it in as you set your final intention to invite your muse into your creative process.

9. Drink and Reflect: Sip the tea slowly, allowing its warmth to fill you. As you drink, remain open to any thoughts, images, or feelings that arise. If inspiration strikes, jot down your insights on the piece of paper.

10. Closing the Ritual: Once you finish your tea, express gratitude for the inspiration and connection you received. You can keep the notes of your insights as a reminder of your communion with the muse.

Repeat this spell whenever you seek creative guidance or inspiration, allowing the unique energy of Aquarius to flow through your artistic endeavors.

Pisces Magic

February 19 - March 20

Pisces Spell: "Dream Weaver"

Ingredients:

- 1 white candle
- 1 small bowl of sea salt
- 1 piece of amethyst or moonstone
- 2 drops of lavender essential oil
- A piece of fabric (preferably blue or silver)

Instructions:

1. Set up your workspace in a calm area, preferably during the night when the moon is visible.

2. Light the white candle to invoke the spiritual and intuitive nature of Pisces.

3. Fill the bowl with sea salt, representing protection and grounding.

4. Place the amethyst or moonstone next to the candle to enhance intuition and dream work.

5. Add two drops of lavender essential oil to the salt, promoting calmness and peaceful dreams.

6. Take the piece of fabric and fold it to create a small pouch.

7. Carefully mix the sea salt and lavender oil

together, then place them inside the pouch along with the amethyst or moonstone.

8.   Hold the pouch in your hands and close your eyes, focusing on your dreams and aspirations. Visualize them coming to fruition.

9.   Once you feel ready, tie the pouch closed and keep it under your pillow or on your nightstand.

10. Allow the candle to burn down completely, knowing that your dreams are being woven into reality.

Spiritual Protection Talisman Spell for Pisces
Ingredients:
*   A small piece of blue or silver cloth (representing water and intuition)
*   A piece of clear quartz (for clarity and protection)
*   A few sprigs of rosemary (for cleansing and protection)
*   A small bowl of salt (for purification)
*   A white candle (for spiritual light and guidance)
*   A small piece of paper and a pen (to write your intention)
Instructions:
1.   Prepare Your Space: Find a quiet place where you can focus without distractions. Cleanse the area by burning sage or incense, or by sprinkling salt around your space.

2.   Set Your Intention: Take the piece of paper and write down your intention for protection. Be specific about what you want to protect yourself from, whether it's negativity, anxiety, or emotional turmoil.

3.   Create the Talisman: Place the blue or silver cloth in front of you. Lay the piece of clear quartz in the center of the cloth. Surround the quartz with the sprigs of rosemary, forming a small circle. Sprinkle a pinch of salt over the quartz and rosemary, symbolizing purification.

4.   Light the Candle: Light the white candle and place it near the talisman setup. As the flame burns, visualize a protective light surrounding you.

5.   Charge the Talisman: Hold your hands over the talisman and say your intention out loud. Envision the protective energy being infused into the quartz, rosemary, and cloth. Allow the warmth of the candle flame to enhance your intention.

6.   Wrap the Talisman: Carefully gather the edges of the cloth to enclose the quartz and rosemary. Tie it with a piece of string or thread, sealing your intention within.

7.   Close the Ritual: Thank any spiritual guides or energies you called upon during the process. Allow the candle to burn down safely, or extinguish it if necessary.

8.   Keep the Talisman: Carry the talisman with you, place it under your pillow, or hang it in your

living space. Whenever you feel the need for protection, hold it in your hands and reaffirm your intention.

Repeat this ritual as needed, especially during times of emotional vulnerability or when you feel negativity around you.

Spell to Remove Negative Energies for Pisces
Ingredients:
- 1 white candle (for purity and protection)
- 1 piece of blue lace agate (for calming energy)
- 1 incense stick or cone of sandalwood (for purification)
- A small bowl of salt (for cleansing)
- A few drops of lavender essential oil (for tranquility)
- A small bowl of water (to represent the water element of Pisces)
- Optional: A few sprigs of fresh rosemary (for protection)

Instructions:
1. Create Your Space: Find a quiet area where you can perform the spell without interruptions. Cleanse the space by opening a window or using a sage smudge stick if you have one.
2. Set Up Your Altar: Place the white candle in the center of your workspace. Arrange the bowl of salt and the bowl of water nearby. Position the blue lace agate and rosemary (if using) around the candle.

3. Light the Candle: As you light the white candle, visualize it burning away any negative energies surrounding you. Say a brief intention, such as, "With this light, I banish negativity and invite peace."

4. Prepare the Incense: Light the sandalwood incense. As the smoke rises, imagine it carrying away any lingering negativity. You can say, "As this incense burns, I release all that no longer serves me."

5. Add Salt to Water: Take a pinch of salt and add it to the bowl of water, stirring gently. As you do this, envision the salt purifying the water and absorbing any remaining negative energies.

6. Anoint with Lavender: Add a few drops of lavender essential oil to your fingertips and gently anoint the blue lace agate. Hold it in your hands, close your eyes, and focus on its calming properties. Visualize a soft blue light surrounding you, creating a protective barrier.

7. Meditate: Sit comfortably and take a few deep breaths. Focus on the flame of the candle and the smoke of the incense. Allow yourself to feel any negativity leaving your body, replaced by a sense of calm and clarity.

8. Conclude the Spell: When you feel ready, thank the energies and elements you have worked with. Allow the candle to burn down safely, and let the incense fully burn out. Dispose of the saltwater mixture outside, symbolizing the release of

negativity.

9. Reflect: Spend a few moments journaling about your experience. Note any feelings, thoughts, or insights that arose during the spell.

This spell can be repeated as needed, especially during times when you feel overwhelmed or affected by negative energies.

Love Spell for Pisces to Find a Deep Connection
Ingredients:
- A pink candle (for love and compassion)
- A blue candle (for emotional depth and intuition)
- A small bowl of water (to represent the water element and emotional connection)
- Rose petals (for romance)
- A piece of rose quartz (for attracting love)
- A few drops of essential oil (like rose or lavender)
- A piece of paper and a pen (to write your intentions)
- A small container or pouch (to keep your ingredients)

Instructions:

1. Create Your Space: Find a quiet, comfortable space where you won't be disturbed. Cleanse the area by lighting some incense or simply visualizing the space filled with white light.

2. Set Up Your Altar: Place the pink and blue

candles on the altar, with the small bowl of water in between them. Scatter the rose petals around the candles and bowl.

3. Prepare Your Intentions: On the piece of paper, write down what you seek in a deep connection. Be specific about the qualities you desire in a partner and the kind of relationship you wish to cultivate.

4. Charge the Rose Quartz: Hold the rose quartz in your hands and close your eyes. Visualize the love and connection you wish to attract. Feel the energy of the stone amplifying your intentions.

5. Anoint the Candles: Use the essential oil to anoint both the pink and blue candles. Start from the base and move upward, visualizing love and emotional depth flowing into the candles.

6. Light the Candles: Light the pink candle first, followed by the blue candle. As you do, say the following incantation (or create your own): "With this flame, I call to thee. Open my heart, let love flow free. A deep connection, pure and true, bring forth the one who's meant for me."

7. Place the Paper: Fold the piece of paper with your intentions and place it under the bowl of water. This symbolizes your emotions carrying your wishes into the universe.

8. Meditate: Spend a few moments in meditation, focusing on the flames and envisioning the deep connection you desire. Feel the energy of

love surrounding you.

9. Close the Ritual: After you feel ready, extinguish the candles (do not blow them out; pinch or snuff them) and thank the universe for the love you are inviting into your life.

10. Keep the Ingredients: Place the rose quartz and the folded paper in the small container or pouch. Keep it in a special place, like under your pillow or on your altar, as a reminder of your intentions.

Repeat this spell as needed, allowing your emotions and intuition to guide you. Trust that the universe is working to bring you the deep connection you seek.

Fast Money Spell for Pisces

Ingredients:

- Green candle (for prosperity)
- Cinnamon (for attraction and abundance)
- A small bowl of salt (for purification)
- A coin (any denomination)
- A piece of paper and pen (to write your intention)
- A small dish of water (to represent the element of water)

Instructions:

1. Create Your Space: Find a quiet place where you won't be disturbed. Set up your ingredients on a clean surface. Light the green candle and place it in front of you.

2.   Purification: Take the bowl of salt and sprinkle a small amount around your workspace, creating a protective barrier. This will help purify the area and enhance the energy of your spell.

3.   Write Your Intention: On the piece of paper, write down your specific intention for attracting money. Be clear and positive (e.g., "I attract fast and abundant financial opportunities").

4.   Cinnamon Power: Sprinkle a pinch of cinnamon over the paper with your intention. As you do this, visualize the energy of abundance flowing into your life.

5.   Coin Offering: Take the coin and hold it in your dominant hand. Close your eyes and focus on the energy of money and abundance. Imagine it flowing freely to you. After a moment, place the coin on top of the paper.

6.   Water Element: Dip your fingers into the dish of water and sprinkle a few drops over the paper and coin, symbolizing flow and abundance. As you do this, say aloud:

"By the power of water and earth,

I call forth wealth, prosperity, and mirth."

1.   Candle Focus: Spend a few moments visualizing your intention as you gaze into the flame of the candle. Imagine it lighting the path to your financial goals.

2.   Seal the Spell: Allow the candle to burn down safely. Once it has burned out, fold the paper with

your intention around the coin and keep it in a special place, like your wallet or a sacred space.

3. Express Gratitude: Thank the universe for the abundance that is on its way to you. Trust that your intention will manifest in the right time and manner.

This spell uses the intuitive and creative energies of Pisces, helping you attract financial opportunities quickly.

Wherever the Stars May Guide You

You are invited to explore the profound interplay between astrology and your personal spiritual practices. For many, astrology serves not only as a tool for self-discovery but also as a guiding light in the realms of witchcraft and ritual. Understanding your astrological sign provides a foundation from which to engage with the universe's energies, allowing you to align your intentions with the cosmic rhythms that govern our lives. This journey is not merely about identifying your zodiac sign; it is an invitation to delve deeper into the unique traits and energies associated with it, transforming these insights into practical applications for spellcasting and personal growth.

Astrological spellcasting is a powerful practice that uses the inherent qualities of each zodiac sign to enhance your magical work. Each sign embodies specific traits, elements, and energies that can be amplified through tailored spells. For instance, a spell focused on manifestation during a lunar phase that aligns with your sign can yield potent results. By including the characteristics of your zodiac sign—such as the assertiveness of Aries or the nurturing energy of Cancer—you can create rituals that resonate deeply with your intentions. This synergy between your sign and your spells not only enhances their effectiveness but also fosters a more profound connection to your astrological essence.

In addition to spellcasting, astrology can be a valuable tool for divination, offering insights into the future and guidance for decision-making. Techniques such as astrological chart readings or horoscope analyses can illuminate the path ahead, revealing opportunities and challenges aligned with cosmic events. By understanding the celestial influences at play, you can make informed choices that resonate with your astrological journey. This predictive aspect of astrology empowers you to navigate life with intention, using the stars as a compass to guide your actions and aspirations.

Astrological rituals for manifestation further amplify the connection between your personal goals and the universe's energies. By aligning your intentions with significant astrological events—like eclipses or planetary transits—you can create powerful rituals that use these cosmic forces. For example, during a full moon in your sign, consider crafting a ritual that focuses on releasing what no longer serves you and inviting in new opportunities. Such practices not only enhance your spiritual development but also serve as a reminder of the cyclical nature of life, encouraging you to embrace change and transformation as part of your journey.

Elemental astrology also plays a crucial role in your exploration of astrological energies. Each zodiac sign is associated with one of the four elements: earth, air, fire, or water, which influences how you interact with the world around you. Understanding these elemental connections can deepen your practice of witchcraft, allowing you to incorporate elemental energies into your spells and rituals. Additionally, specific crystals and gemstones resonate with each zodiac sign, offering unique properties that can enhance your magical work. By identifying and utilizing these stones, you can create a harmonious environment that supports your astrological journey, empowering you to embrace your true self and manifest your desires with confidence.

The Ongoing Relationship Between Astrology and Witchcraft

The relationship between astrology and witchcraft is both ancient and intricate, deeply rooted in the belief systems and practices of various cultures throughout history. Both disciplines share a common foundation in the understanding of cosmic energies and the influence these energies exert on human lives. Astrology provides a framework for understanding the celestial movements and their implications, while witchcraft offers practical tools for using these energies to manifest desires, create change, and engage with the spiritual realm. Together, they form a powerful synergy that enhances the practices of both astrologers and practitioners of witchcraft.

Astrological spellcasting is one area where the two practices intersect significantly. Each zodiac sign embodies unique traits and energies that can be amplified through specific spells tailored to those characteristics. For instance, a spell designed for Aries may focus on courage and initiative, while a spell for Pisces might center around intuition and emotional healing. By aligning spells with the astrological influences of the moment, practitioners can increase their effectiveness, making the magic more resonant and potent. This alignment not only respects the natural rhythms of the universe but also allows individuals to work in harmony with their own astrological makeup.

Divination is another realm where astrology and witchcraft converge. Astrological charts serve as a rich source of information for predictive techniques, offering insights into potential future events and personal challenges. Practitioners can blend traditional divination methods, such as tarot or scrying, with astrological insights to deepen their understanding of the messages being conveyed. This fusion of practices enriches the divinatory process, allowing individuals to interpret the signs and symbols of their lives through both cosmic and earthly lenses. By recognizing the interplay between celestial events and personal fate, practitioners can better navigate their journey.

Astrological rituals for manifestation are particularly potent during significant astrological events, such as eclipses or planetary transits. These moments are charged with energy, making them ideal for setting intentions or performing rituals aimed at personal growth and transformation. For example, a new moon ritual may focus on intentions for new beginnings, while a full moon ceremony could be centered on release and letting go. By including the timing of these celestial occurrences into their practices, individuals can capitalize on the amplified energies, aligning their personal aspirations with the greater cosmic cycles.

Elemental astrology adds another layer to the relationship between astrology and witchcraft, as it emphasizes the four classical elements—earth, air, fire, and water—and their associations with the zodiac signs. Each element carries its own unique qualities and correspondences, influencing how practitioners approach their magical work. For instance, earth signs like Taurus and Capricorn may resonate with stability and material abundance, while fire signs such as Leo and Sagittarius may evoke passion and creativity. By understanding these elemental connections, practitioners can select appropriate rituals, spells, and even crystals that align with their zodiac sign, enhancing their effectiveness in magical workings. Thus, the ongoing relationship between astrology and witchcraft creates a rich tapestry of practices that empower individuals on their spiritual journeys.

Encouragement for Continued Practice and Exploration

As you delve deeper into the realms of astrology and witchcraft, remember that both are journeys rich with layers of knowledge and personal discovery. Each zodiac sign offers unique traits and energies that can enhance your spiritual practices, making it essential to continue exploring how these celestial influences intersect with your everyday life. By embracing the wisdom of your sign and its corresponding rituals, you can cultivate a more profound connection to the universe, enhancing your spellcasting and divination practices. Allow this subchapter to serve as a gentle reminder that the path of astrological exploration is one that flourishes with consistent practice and an open heart.

Continued engagement with astrological principles can greatly enrich your understanding of the cosmos and your place within it. Each planetary transit, lunar phase, and solar event presents a unique opportunity for personal growth and transformation. By observing these celestial occurrences and aligning your rituals with them, you can use their energy to manifest your desires. Consider establishing a regular practice of tracking astrological events in a journal, noting how they influence your emotions and experiences. This will not only enhance your spellcasting but also deepen your intuitive connection to the universe.

Exploration is not just about learning; it is also about experimentation. Dive into the world of astrological divination techniques to uncover insights about your future or gain clarity on present challenges. Whether you choose to work with natal charts, transits, or lunar cycles, each method offers distinct perspectives that can lead to profound revelations. Remember that the art of divination is as much about interpretation as it is about the tools you use. Trust your intuition and allow it to guide you through your astrological explorations, for often the most significant insights come from within.

The relationship between astrology and the four elements—earth, air, fire, and water—is fundamental to both your astrological practice and your witchcraft. Each zodiac sign is associated with one of these elements, which influences not only personality traits but also the effectiveness of specific spells and rituals. By understanding how these elements interact with your sign, you can tailor your practices to resonate more harmoniously with the energies at play. Incorporate elemental associations into your rituals, utilizing the grounding nature of earth, the intellectual clarity of air, the passionate drive of fire, or the emotional depth of water to enhance your magical workings.

Finally, do not underestimate the power of crystals and gemstones in your astrological practice. Each zodiac sign corresponds to specific stones that amplify their inherent qualities, making them invaluable tools for healing, protection, and manifestation. As you continue your journey, explore the diverse properties of these gemstones and integrate them into your rituals and spellcasting. Whether you carry them as talismans, place them on your altar, or use them in meditative practices, their energy will support your exploration of astrology and witchcraft. Embrace the ongoing journey of practice and exploration, for in every moment lies an opportunity to deepen your understanding and connection to the universe.

About the Author

Emeleth Morliniel holds a Third Degree in British Celtic Traditional Witchcraft. That's a fancy way of saying she spent a lot of years in witch school and underwent a lot of initiation and elevation rites, and is now considered qualified to carry out the role of High Priestess. But within her own Circle, she's usually the one managing the group's energy work and spellcraft because she's exceedingly bad at memorizing lines.